About the Book

John Frémont, nick-named *The Pathfinder*, travelled among Indians and Mountain Men as he trailblazed his way across the American continent in the 1840's. Many of the adventures he and his good friend and guide, Kit Carson, shared are told in this biography. Frémont's explorations for the army across the uncharted Rockie Mountains and the treacherous Sierra Nevadas opened the West to settlement by thousands of Americans who soon followed the trails he found. Their occupation of the land west of the mountains helped to secure California Territory for the United States.

William Orr's handsome illustrations add greatly to the text and reflect painstaking research — even to the type of rifles Frémont's men carried.

Fort Vancouver
Columbia
River
Snake River
1843-44
Fremont Peak
South Pass
Salt Lake
Fort Bridger
Platte RIVE
18
Monterey
1843-44
Pikes Peak
Bent's Fort
Kansas Riv
Arkansas R
Missouri River
C

JOHN CHARLES FRÉMONT

ADVENTURER IN THE WILDERNESS

BY VADA F. CARLSON

ILLUSTRATED BY WILLIAM A. ORR

HARVEY HOUSE, INC.
Publishers
Irvington-on-Hudson, N.Y. 10533

Library of Congress Catalog Card Number 79-148109
Manufactured in the United States of America
ISBN 0-8178-4961-0, Trade Edition. ISBN 0-8178-4962-9, Library Edition

Harvey House, Inc. *Publishers*
Irvington, New York 10533

Contents

1	A Lover of Action	9
2	A Surveyor at Seventeen	19
3	In Sioux Territory	38
4	A Stormy Romance	61
5	On the Trail with Carson	75
6	A National Hero	104
7	"Sutter's Fort's Ahead!"	121
8	Another Honor Conferred	137
9	Heartbreaking Days	151
10	He Had Served His Country Well	163
	Bibliography	171
	Index	173

1

A Lover of Action

JOHN CHARLES FRÉMONT's big black eyes sparkled with excitement. His father, just back from a trip into the wilderness, was unrolling a map and spreading it out on the table.

Quietly John Charles rose from his stool beside the fireplace. With his purring kitten in his arms, he tiptoed to the table and edged in between his pretty mother and his tanned and bearded father, both of whom were bent over the worn map.

By craning his thin neck, he could see the marks on the map that meant rivers and creeks, but it was to the sketches of Indians, drawn around the map's edges, that his eyes were drawn in fascination.

What wild-looking people those Indians were, he thought. How much fun they must have, dressing up with feathers and beads and dancing to the beat of tom-toms.

"This is the French-Indian trapper I told you about," John Charles' father said, pointing to a sketch of a man with a notched ear and a scar on his cheek. "An arrow almost ended his career. He's a wonderful storyteller, Anne. He's been out on the Great Plains beyond the Missouri River, he says. He says there are many Indian tribes out there. Plenty of game and herds of buffalo. Herds that fill whole valleys. I'll take you there someday."

"When the children are old enough to travel," Mrs. Frémont said, "perhaps we can all get a glimpse of these faraway places you love so much."

"I'm old enough now," John Charles piped up, looking up at them, big-eyed and serious.

Charles Frémont smiled at his son who looked so much like him, and ruffled the boy's black curls.

"Five is a little young," he said. "But, who knows? You may grow up to see much more of the West than I've seen."

"You were told to go to bed," John Charles' mother reminded the boy gently. "Don't you remember?"

"Yes, ma'am," John Charles sighed. "But . . . oh, please, Mother, let me stay just a little longer. I like to hear Father tell about the Indians and the rivers and — and everything."

His father chuckled.

"Let him stay," he said. "His interest pleases me."

John Charles stayed and listened. His father, who earned a very poor living for his family by teaching French and art, talked on and on. There was a place, he said, called St. Louis. The fur trappers met there before setting out for the creeks and rivers and lakes where the beaver and the muskrat and the mink were to be found.

John Charles' mind was filled with the magic of the outdoors as he climbed slowly up the stairs to the bedrooms. The moon was making a path across his bed.

"Like a river," John Charles whispered, pulling the covers over himself. "A silvery river in the wilderness."

He closed his eyes, but his father's voice seemed to echo in his ears, saying, "Mississippi, the queen of rivers . . . The silvery Missouri . . . St. Louis . . ."

His father, that restless Frenchman, had never been content to stay in one place for long, but John

Charles knew only the life of the Southland. Both before and following John Charles' birth in Savannah, the Frémonts had moved frequently. Now they had made another move, this time to the city of Richmond, in Virginia.

Richmond was the birthplace of his mother. Her father had been a colonel — Colonel Thomas Whiting. She had many relatives in Richmond.

She had relatives, too, in Charleston, South Carolina. When John Charles' father died, she was persuaded to move to Charleston and to make a home there for John Charles, his sister, and his infant brother.

John Charles, just six years old, was enrolled in school in Charleston. He loved school. Learning was easy for him. He could not learn everything he wanted to know fast enough. Soon he was at the head of his class.

His interest in school continued all through the lower grades.

"Your son is especially good in arithmetic," one of his teachers told his mother as John Charles neared his teens. "However, it's not easy to keep him busy. I give him an assignment, and in minutes he has solved all his problems. Correctly, too, may

I add. Then . . . well, he gets into mischief. He's a very active youngster."

"Mischief? What does he do?" his mother asked.

"Talks. Teases the others. Twits them for being so slow. Things like that," the teacher reported.

John Charles' mother began to worry about her son's future. Intellect such as this deserved higher training than elementary schools could provide, but she had no money to pay for higher instruction. Yet, it would be a shame to prevent the boy from growing into the brilliant person he might well become with college training.

She talked to some of her influential friends. They agreed that John Charles should go to college, and they offered to help with his education.

A lawyer, who knew the family and who liked John Charles, was especially interested.

"You have given him good home training," he told Mrs. Frémont. "He has perfect manners and a great deal of personal charm, as well as more than his share of good looks. It might be good for him to spend a year in my office, reading law. I have a very good library, you know."

John Charles was happy to know that he could

continue his education, but at the same time he dreaded being cooped up in a dingy little office filled with shelves of musty lawbooks.

Like most boys his age, he was a good horseman. He spent much of his leisure time riding in the country, which he found infinitely more interesting than the city.

Secretly he had been dreaming of joining some westbound caravan and journeying to St. Louis, where surely some group of explorers would need his services. The glinting rivers, the uncluttered

spaces, the freedom of the great West his father had talked about still held first place in his mind.

But he did not rebel. He knew he had a responsibility to his family and that legal training might help him later on. Nonetheless, he felt trapped and often looked out the window with longing.

Dr. Charles Robertson, who tutored promising boys for college entrance, was a friend of John W. Mitchell, the lawyer in whose office John Charles was now spending a great deal of his time.

He met John Charles and became interested in him.

"I'm surprised at his ability, especially in mathematics," he told the lawyer. "He *must* go to college. He should be studying Greek and Latin, right now. And higher mathematics. Bring him to me."

This was a pleasant surprise to John Charles. He liked the advanced work that Dr. Robertson taught. Latin and Greek were easy for him to learn and to understand. Besides, it was a pleasure to have other boys of his own type in his classes.

Dr. Robertson was elated.

"That young friend of yours will be ready for

college this fall," he told the lawyer.

"Come, now!" said the lawyer. "He's only fourteen!"

"I know that," Robertson agreed. "He's young, but he'll be ready. I'm certain that he can skip the freshman classes and enter as a sophomore — if not a junior! He'd make a splendid teacher. He likes to help others."

"But he's such a small lad," the lawyer pointed out.

"Yes, he is small for his age, but he's a healthy fellow. He's wiry and strong in spite of his small-boned body and his refined features. Never fear. He'll command respect wherever he goes," the teacher predicted.

Mrs. Frémont was overjoyed by the report. She had always respected her son's quick mind. Now others were recognizing it. She talked to John Charles about training to teach school.

John Charles brushed his dark curls back from his forehead and shook his head.

"A teacher? Cooped up in a schoolroom all day long? I don't believe I'd like that very much. I'm too much like Father. I want to be free. I want to explore wild places; see what goes on in the wild

places to the west of the Mississippi River. I want
to set my foot on spots that no other white man has
touched. I want to make trails through the wilderness and have maps to show the stay-at-homes, just
as Father did, though few would study them."

It was flattering to be thought well of, but John
Charles was more sad than pleased. Everyone
seemed to want him to be something he had no
desire to be.

However, he did want to go to college. To his
mother's surprise and satisfaction, he entered
Charleston College at the beginning of the fall
term. As Dr. Robertson had predicted, he did not
enter as a freshman. Instead, he skipped both
freshman and sophomore classes and entered as a
junior!

He was fast growing up. Though he was not a
large young man, he had a mature manner. No one
called him John Charles now, except his mother.
He was John to his classmates and other friends.
He was quiet and a trifle withdrawn, but his manners reflected his mother's cultured background,
and he was interested in people, plants, animals,
and the earth in general — lakes, rivers, mountains,
deserts. The outdoors called to him.

2

A Surveyor at Seventeen

JOHN WAS A SENIOR in Charleston College when he
met Cecilia, a flashing-eyed, laughing Creole girl
about his own age, and the sister of two of his
friends.

He had borrowed a canoe that day and was
paddling up one of the many creeks of the South
Carolina countryside when he saw her and her
brothers cooking something over a little fire on the
bank of the stream.

Their boat was tied to a tree nearby, and the three of them hailed him, urging him to join them for a fish dinner.

He accepted and spent the rest of the day with them, hearing again the story of how they barely escaped being massacred by Indians after a sudden uprising of a Louisiana tribe.

This was the free, unhampered life that John had dreamed of. These Creole youngsters were

doing what he yearned to do. As he joined them more and more often in exploration of the waterways, his college work began to suffer.

For the first time he fancied himself in love.

His teachers scolded him. Dr. Robertson scolded him. His mother reproached him for his lack of interest to graduate with honors.

Each time, feeling guilty because he preferred being with Cecilia and her brothers to attending classes, he studied hard. It was not difficult for him to catch up with the class, but the beautiful outdoors was foremost in his mind those spring days. Suddenly, he would fail to attend class.

Like a wild bird escaped from its cage, he would fly to his happy-go-lucky friends.

The patience of the college authorities wore thin. They called him in, lectured him severely, and expelled him from college.

His mother was greatly disappointed. She went to the dean and begged him to reconsider the matter.

"Please give him another chance," she urged. "I'm sure I can get him to work harder."

The dean shook his head.

"Mrs. Frémont, it is not that John does not work

hard — when he honors us with his presence. It is simply that he lacks respect for authority," the dean pointed out. "He wants his own way — all the time. He needs to learn the value of discipline."

It was almost a relief to John to be expelled from college. But the thought of his responsibility for his mother's welfare could not be brushed aside. How was he to earn money for her needs? He would have graduated in another few weeks. Perhaps he should have spent less time with Cecilia and her brothers.

All that night John's thoughts ran round and round. He would have to find a way to earn money.

He had been told that he would make a good teacher. Very well, then, perhaps he could pick up a few boys to tutor, and in that way pay the bills at home.

He had no difficulty in getting pupils, but now he was really "cooped up" day in and day out, and he disliked this means of making money intensely.

Again, without being asked, the lawyer friend, Attorney Mitchell, came to his aid.

"I need your help, John," he said one day. "The outcome of a lawsuit depends on the survey of my client's rice field. Will you survey it for me? I know you can do it."

"I've never surveyed anything," John replied, "but I know how it should be done. Yes, I'll do it."

His mother objected.

"No, John. It's too dangerous. There are clouds of mosquitoes in that swampy area. You'll die of malaria. And, besides, everyone knows there are deadly copperheads in the marsh. You'd be risking your life."

"I'm not afraid," John reassured her, busy with his preparations. "There are all sorts of dangers in living. I'll survive."

Why should he worry about mosquitoes and snakes, when he intended to be off to the wilderness at the first opportunity? Out there he'd be braving hostile Indians, raging rivers, snowy mountains, dim trails, and wild animals. Compared to those dangers, it seemed a little foolish to worry about surveying a rice field in his own Southland. He had no fears as he saddled his horse and rode out into the country.

That night he had to admit that his mother's prediction had been all too true. He was covered with mosquito bites, and a copperhead had actually slithered across his path, making him stand still for a moment, and half decide to give up the task as too dangerous.

When he was getting netting to drape over his hat the next day, he was glad he had not allowed himself to be scared by the insects and the snakes of the marsh. Mosquitoes! Snakes! Mere nothings to an explorer, and besides, wasn't he learning a useful occupation?

The landowner was delighted with the speed and accuracy of John's surveying.

"That seventeen-year old is a born surveyor," he told his friends. This generous praise led to an assignment with a surveying crew working at that time in the Charleston area.

Now John was able to spend more time with his Creole friends. They hunted in the woods. They went sailing, sometimes venturing so far to seaward that they were in danger of being swamped by breakers. And always, as he enjoyed the water, the woods, and the fields, there was that inner urge to be up and away to the frontier.

After the surveying was finished, he went to work in the Apprentices' Library in Charleston. One afternoon he discovered a book that was to influence his life.

It was *Expedition to the Upper Mississippi,* by Henry R. Schoolcraft.

He picked the book up idly and flipped the pages, stopping when he came to a beautifully drawn map. Forgetting everything else, he studied the map. That night he carried the book home with him.

It was a large book and contained many maps. He was still reading and studying at three o'clock the next morning. He scarcely realized that time was passing, until his mother tapped at his door.

"Are you ill, Son?" she called anxiously. "Or did you just fall asleep without blowing out your light?"

John laughed.

"Come in, Mother. . . . No, I'm not ill. I have never felt better. See this book? It's helped me to make a firm decision. I shall explore the West. Others are already in the field doing this work. Schoolcraft has mapped the Mississippi River Basin; I want to map the Missouri's basin. Oh, Mother! I feel that my *real* life is just beginning."

From then on he began looking forward to traveling, and when he was almost twenty, the opportunity came.

When John was sixteen, he had become acquainted with a South Carolinian named Joel Roberts Poinsett. Poinsett was of French Huguenot descent and enjoyed conversing in French with John. Usually their subject was botany, in which John was very much interested.

Poinsett had been United States minister to Mexico, after representing the Government in South America. During his stay in Mexico he became interested in a showy Mexican flower. His articles about it were widely read, and the flower was named after him, *Poinsettia.*

When John was asked to teach mathematics to midshipmen aboard the training sloop of war, *Natchez,* he asked Mr. Poinsett to recommend him. The *Natchez* was to make a cruise of three years along the coast of South America, visiting all the important cities en route. John felt that this experience would give him a good idea of that country, while at the same time, he was being paid to teach a subject in which he excelled.

Poinsett recommended John for the position, though he felt that it was not particularly good for his young friend, especially since the freedom-loving young man would be "cooped up" on the ship in a way he did not quite realize.

John thought that the position would only de-

lay his frontier explorations for a time. It was the salary that interested him.

By that time John was a fully matured young man. He was slender and handsome; he looked splendid in his uniform, and he was a person that both men and women were attracted to at once. He seemed older than he was, because he had studied Greek and Latin, spoke French fluently, and was well-read in many subjects, including law, botany, Indians, and the study of the earth's surface.

Although he was sure of his ability to teach mathematics, it was not easy to stand before the midshipmen, many of whom were older than he was. Most of them were also both taller and heavier. They snickered openly when he was introduced as their teacher.

Their snickers were soon stopped. John was a strict teacher. He demanded discipline, and he received it.

Fortunately, there was no one aboard to tell his students what a rebel he had been.

Once they accepted him, they began to like him. John relaxed into his usual friendliness and, though he gave them long, hard assignments, he made lessons interesting with stories. Along with their arithmetic the midshipmen were given large doses of ancient history. John was a good storyteller; he had a magnificent voice, and this spice helped to make the long study sessions endurable.

It was not long before John realized that Poinsett was right in advising him against this teaching assignment. True, the *Natchez* put in at colorful ports. Also, he was learning to deal with men, as he would have to do if he ever headed an exploring unit. But the life aboard a ship was a restraint that he did not enjoy. Often, as he stood at the rail and looked off to the far horizon, he wished he were back on land, paddling up a friendly little stream or riding horseback through woods where birds sang and squirrels chattered.

There was no escaping his duty, however, so he went about it with his customary vigor. His work was done so well and so thoroughly that it brought praise from both U.S. Navy and government officials.

When the cruise ended, he was offered a commission of professor of mathematics in the Navy, and he agreed to take an examination for the post. He passed the test easily. However, before he accepted the commission, something more to his liking was offered.

The United States Topographical Engineers' Corps needed a good map maker to help to survey a route for a railroad from Charleston, South Carolina, to Cincinnati, Ohio.

John gave up the commission and a career in the Navy for this new venture. He had dreamed of this kind of job for years.

Adding to his happiness at that time was the action of Charleston College. His exploits had not been unnoticed by the authorities. In spite of his disagreement with them, they realized that he had distinguished himself. They forgave him for skipping classes and for lacking discipline, and gave him a degree.

Surveying in the mountains of western South Carolina and Tennessee was not *exactly* what he had dreamed about. There were no real dangers or hardships to be faced in that area. The weather was mild and agreeable, and no different from that he had known all his life. But at least, he was living the outdoor life he had longed for, and he was learning more about surveying. This, he thought, was his right place in life and like being paid for taking a pleasant vacation.

The one trouble was that it did not last long. Because he had been so pleasantly engaged, and had been devoted to the task assigned to him, the time seemed to fly. Soon, that task finished, he was back at home in Charleston, impatiently waiting for news of the next assignment.

The order came very soon. This time Captain W. S. Williams needed John's help to make a military examination of Cherokee Indian country.

Indian country! The words thrilled the young man. He thought of his father. Charles Frémont had often talked about the Cherokees and had made many sketches of their faces. John looked forward to working among them, learning their ways, and making friends with them.

When the Williams party arrived at the Cherokee village, where the survey was to begin, they found the Cherokee men in an unfriendly mood. To talk to them was impossible. To stay among them might prove highly dangerous. They had been feasting and drinking all day. They would need time to sleep off the spree before they would be able to talk sense.

The Indian women were worried. They did not want trouble with this military group. They talked together, then they told Williams that they would hide his men for the night.

They led the way to an old tumble-down log hut which had been used for storing corn. There Williams, John, and the others rolled up in their blankets and tried to sleep.

Sleep was impossible. The howling of the Indian men continued all night long. There were fights, too, with grunts and screams and shouts of anger. Besides, rats prowled the hut, running over the men and giving them more concern than did the Indians.

With daylight came quiet. The Cherokee men were asleep in their huts.

"Let's get rid of the rat smells," Williams said. He and John went to the river, on the bank of which the village had been built, and jumped in for an icy, stimulating bath. Then they ate a hearty breakfast and began their work.

"You will take on the task of exploring the Hiwassee," Williams told John, and John nodded agreement, as he liked the idea. He would have an opportunity to talk to the Indians, to observe them at work and at play. In this way they would not be lumped as a tribe, but would become individuals, with personal characteristics and names.

John was interested in people—not just certain

people who were approved by society, but people as a whole. He was interested in what these people thought; why they thought that way; how they reacted to situations, especially those calling for courage.

As he worked along the pretty little Hiwassee, his eyes were opened to the very human traits of the Cherokees. They did quarrel at times. They did fight each other savagely. They did endure terrible pain without crying out. They did prefer peace, but they would not run from hand-to-hand combat. They were more afraid of the "spirits" which they thought ran around in the dark than they were of human beings, Indian or otherwise.

The Cherokees were as complex as any other race of people. They were not romantic, and they did not live the idyllic life he had imagined. But he found them to be cooperative friends and companions, expert woodsmen, intelligent farmers.

From the Cherokee young men who were often his companions during the survey, he learned how to protect himself in the forest; how to keep his directions straight by observing tree growth and other natural signs placed by nature. He learned the Indian way of survival in time of famine.

When his work of exploring the sparkling Hiwassee was finished, he was ready for the next
call; it was not long in coming.

His friend, Joel Poinsett, had been named Secretary of War by President Martin Van Buren.
Through his influence, John Charles Frémont was
appointed second lieutenant in the United States
Topographical Engineers' Corps.

His mother gave him the news when he returned to Charleston, and she told him he was ordered to report at once to the War Department in
Washington.

Secretary Poinsett greeted John warmly, plainly
approving his neat, soldierly appearance in his
new blue uniform with its shining gold braid.

"I know you have had no military training,

John," the older man said, "but you look every inch
the soldier I know you are. We have a great need
for capable, keen, young men just now. This is an
era of tremendous possibilities for the United
States. This is an era of expansion. West of the
Mississippi and along the reaches of the Missouri
there is a vast region, unexplored by white men.
This must be done, and soon."

"Thank you, sir," John said, his eyes glinting
with excitement and eagerness to be on his way at
last to the real wilderness of the West. "When do
we start?"

"As soon as plans can be completed," Poinsett
told him, pleased with the young man's eagerness.
"You have heard of Joseph Nicholas Nicollet? He's
the famous French astronomer and geologist. He
will head the expedition, and it will be an honor to
work with him, I'm certain.

"Ferdinand R. Hassler, the Swiss surveyor—ah,
I see you've heard of him, too—will be in the party.

"We feel that you, John, are the logical young
man to assist Nicollet. Mapping the huge Missouri
River Basin will be an important undertaking. It
must be accomplished with exactness."

John's spirits soared. He seemed almost to be

growing taller as he thought of the mission ahead. The Missouri Basin! He remembered the night he had forgotten time and space while reading *Expedition to the Upper Mississippi*. He remembered with what conviction he had told his mother that he would explore the West.

"I appreciate your faith in me," John told the Secretary, his voice steady, though he felt his heart racing. "Thank you for this great opportunity."

So starry-eyed that he hardly knew what he was doing, he left the Secretary's office. How he wished for a good friend with whom he could share this moment!

He thought of Cecilia and her brothers. They would be the ideal listeners, but he no longer knew where they were, and he had no friends, except Poinsett, in the capital city.

As he walked along Pennsylvania Avenue in his fresh new uniform, he was a very lonely young man. He had no love for cities. This city, with its hustle and bustle and noise, was a strange place, a foreign scene. He would have felt more at home on the banks of the Hiwassee, among the Cherokees.

As he thought of that period, he lost his glumness and felt transported. He could hear the bird songs. He could feel the breeze flowing through the forest; smell the dampness of the earth and the pungent odor of growing things. It was not difficult to imagine the throb of a distant drum and the far-off falsetto voices of singers.

For a flash, time ceased to be. Then, coming back to reality, John set his jaw in determination.

"I'll give them service," he vowed. "Real service. The very best!"

He was impressed by Joseph Nicholas Nicollet, leader of the proposed expedition. One had only to watch his movements to know that there would be no slipshod work under his command. He would be exact. Nothing but the best would please Nicollet.

"I am equal to the task," John told himself, lifting his chin and squaring his shoulders. "Whatever is in store for me, I shall meet it with strength and courage."

One trial he had to meet immediately was inactivity. He was a restless young man during the few weeks that he lived in Washington waiting for the order to join Nicollet and Hassler, who had gone on to St. Louis.

3

In Sioux Territory

St. Louis! After experiencing Washington, with its political atmosphere, St. Louis was very welcome to twenty-four-year-old Lieutenant John Charles Frémont. There was hustle and bustle here as well as in Washington, but it was of a very different kind—the western kind that sent John's blood racing through his veins in mad delight.

St. Louis was the jumping-off place for the wilderness which he had so long imagined. The

people here had none of the polished look of east-
erners. Even Nicollet and Hassler had the look of
the West.

As for the fur trappers and the traders, the
French-Canadian and Indian guides, and the men
and women who were to make up the emigrant
trains—these were a people apart.

The river boats came whistling in; sternwheel-
ers churned up the muddy water. There was a
great scurry of loading and unloading: the boats
going out carrying supplies; those coming in bring-
ing bales of smelly furs from the wilderness.

Lieutenant Frémont was interested in every
sight, sound, and smell. Like a thirsty man, he
drank them all in through his eyes, ears, and nose.
This was a part of the life he had longed for and
was soon to experience to the fullest.

The trappers and traders, long away from civ-
ilization, were as eager to talk as he himself had
been in Washington. They answered his questions,
seeming to be pleased to have an excuse for telling
about their experiences, which were sometimes
tragic, but more often humorous. Each one gave
him a new vision of what he might expect "out
there."

From all these accounts he began to see the expedition for what it would be: one of many dangers, but also one of many rewarding experiences. He was filled with a great impatience to start, to begin to live his own experiences, whatever these were going to be.

Nicollet knew many people in St. Louis and took pleasure in introducing his young assistant to them.

"You have a great gift for making friends," he told John one day. "You will find this gift invaluable to you in the work you will be doing. I have found that people seem to want to help those who are friendly and helpful to them. You find them interesting; you listen—*really listen*—to what they have to say, and they open up like books. They spill out a treasure trove of frontier knowledge. Oh, one learns much by listening."

Finally, when all the preparations had been made, and the information that they would need had been obtained, they boarded the river boat that would take them upstream.

In order to survey and map the huge territory lying north of the Missouri River, Nicollet had made plans to conduct two surveys in that area. He had already surveyed the upper Mississippi River area. The present survey would connect with this former one and would continue westward to the watershed of the Missouri. The next one would be a survey of the Upper Missouri.

The point from which they started on this second expedition was a frontier trading post on the west bank of the Mississippi at the mouth of the Minnesota River. The fur trader there was friendly. The surveyors had now entered the homeland of

the Sioux Indians, whom the trader knew well. He briefed the party on the Sioux and their attitude at that time about the invasion of white men, even unarmed surveying teams.

One Sioux tribe lived in a village nearby. With others of the party John visited the encampment, and met one of the most beautiful Indian girls he was ever to see. Her name in English was "Beautiful Day," and she was so lovely that he never forgot her.

The young lieutenant saw that there was much to be learned in this new country. It was totally unlike his Southland. The miles between St. Louis and this frontier trading post were not many, but young Frémont felt that he might as well have been lifted out of the United States and into some strange, foreign scene.

At the river the land was not too rugged for the one-horse carts of the expedition. When they left the Mississippi and began journeying along the Minnesota River, John enjoyed the fertile country-side and the picturesque tall tepees of the Sioux people. The Sioux Indians were different, he observed, from the Cherokees. They were big-boned, strong-featured people, whose direct gaze was proof of their fearlessness. He admired them and their independent mode of living.

The buffalo, he soon discovered, was vitally important to them. From the buffalo hides they made the covering for their conical homes. The hides, which the Sioux women softened, were also sewn into handsome robes for the women and into men's attire for the braves. For ornamentation they used flattened and dyed quills of the porcupines, elk teeth, and trading-post beads.

The buffalo, likewise, provided their main food. The big hump of the shaggy animal was the choice cut, but every part of it was used in some manner. Even the bones were boiled, and the marrow from them was eaten.

The Sioux were masters in the art of using the products of nature. Even the buffalo dung was used for fires when the Indians were on the prairie and far from wood of any kind. They also wove baskets from pliant willows and reeds, and they treated their illnesses with herbs and roots.

Women's work in a Sioux tepee was never-ending. The men, on the other hand, went on forays, stealing horses from the trappers and other westbound white men, fighting with bands from other tribes, and killing animals for meat for the families in the encampments.

When days were too cold for these pursuits, the men fashioned arrows and spears from flint, learned to shoot the rifles of the white men, made peace pipes and tomahawks from red pipestone, and pogamoggans—those deadly clubs made of stone fastened to a slender handle—that could crush a man's skull with one blow.

The expeditionary forces crossed to the north bank of the Minnesota at its bend, a place near which settlers later built a town named for Nicollet. Then they traveled on to the mouth of the Cottonwood River, crossed it and explored it to its source.

They planned to follow this stream to its head-waters, where they would find a red pipestone quarry, long used by the northern Indians. This quarry, now a National Monument, was easily found because of the worn trails that led directly to it, showing that the Indians had known about it and used it for many years, perhaps centuries.

Lieutenant Frémont, whose interest in Indians and their ways continued to grow, went into the quarry and chipped off a small specimen of the bright red rock for his collection. It was fine-grained stone, he could see, and readily workable into peace pipes and other articles.

"Nature seems to be in favor of this expedition," he told Nicollet. "So far the weather has been delightful. These river valleys are beautiful, and the night sky—I've never seen the stars so bright. Our astronomical calculations are made with no problems at all. Can it possibly be more beautiful farther west?"

"Wait," Nicollet advised him. "Wait until you see the Rockies!"

But the Rockies were not to be visited on that expedition. Instead, they made a short visit to a friend of Nicollet. This man, Joseph Renville, ran an isolated trading post. He was part Indian and knew the tribes and their habits. They talked with him for hours, learning a great deal about what they might expect from Indians of his area.

These Indians were not the roving, and often starving, people they had been before the time of the fur trappers. Now they sold their furs and buffalo robes, buying white man's clothing, beads and baubles, and watered-down white man's whisky, as well as flour, sugar, coffee, and other foods which they had learned to like.

The men of the expedition then turned east again, continuing to the Minnesota River, but mapping the Blue Earth River drainage area and that of smaller streams in the process.

They camped again at the mouth of the Minnesota. The main expedition prepared to return to St. Louis, and Nicollet would then go on to Washington City.

Lieutenant Frémont would have gone with the others, except for the lure of going on a hunting trip with men from the fur-trading post. The Sioux

Indians, who were camped nearby, were going along. It would, Frémont knew, be a terrific experience for a greenhorn such as he then was. He bought a good hunting horse, crammed his saddlebags with provisions, and joined the group.

It was November. The winter snows had not yet begun, but the air was crisp. It would be perfect for hard riding, should that be necessary. Lieutenant Frémont hoped to kill a buffalo—his first.

From the first, they found elk and deer plentiful.

"They've come down from the mountains," one of the men from the post explained. "They get out before the deep snows fall. Wild things show a lot of sense. More than people do, sometimes."

The young man from Charleston enjoyed every moment of the excursion. The men were friendly. There was always venison to be cooked over the evening campfires. There were many streams of clear, sweet water. The horses found plenty of grass to eat. The Indians sang and danced at night, their tom-toms throbbing in the moonlight.

One evening Frémont saw a glow off to the south. He pointed to it and asked one of the men. "What's that?"

"Prairie fire," the man said. "Grass is dry now. Fires start easy. Sometimes Injuns set 'em, so the new grass can come up faster, I guess. Anyhow, no worry. The wind's taking it away from us."

With his artistic and poetic temperament, it was natural that John would notice the pictures the Indian women presented as they roasted meat over the evening fires. He tried to sketch them, but found that he did not have his father's artistic talent.

They rode from early dawn until late afternoon, ate well, slept well in spite of increasingly cold weather, but returned to camp without having caught a glimpse of the buffalo herds they had hoped to find.

"I'm not too disappointed," he told his friends as he boarded the boat that would take him to St. Louis. "We'll be coming back in the spring if plans work out. I'll get my buffalo then."

Winter was on his heels as he rejoined the men at St. Louis. Soon there was heavy snow and ice, but there was no slacking up of the work of the exploring party. New men experienced in frontier life were hired. Additional equipment was purchased, and passage on a river boat was booked, in order to be sure that the entire group could take off at the same time.

The men who had stayed at the trading post were to meet the expedition at the mouth of the James River, in the southeast corner of present-day South Dakota. The actual work of exploration and mapping was to begin at Fort Pierre.

The main party started by boat from St. Louis on schedule in the spring, but they did not reach Fort Pierre as early as they had hoped. There had been heavy snows in the high country; now the snows were melting and pouring water down the small streams and into the Missouri River. The little river boat fought its way upstream against the raging water. At times it could barely hold its position, let alone make headway.

At one time they ran aground on a sandbar that had been swept in with the spring flow. Another time they were hampered by trees that had been uprooted by flooding and had been carried into the mainstream.

At still another point their progress was held up for an hour or more because a herd of buffalo was crossing the river.

They made less than twenty miles a day, and it was seventy days before they reached the dock at Fort Pierre.

One of the first problems Nicollet faced there was getting approval of the Indians. This was Sioux territory. There were many tribes of Sioux, each with its own chief and its own opinion of the white man. This particular band was friendly, but talks would be necessary before the men of the expedition could fan out over the area.

With the aid of the trader, talks between Nicollet and the chieftains were arranged. These talks could not be held in the brisk way of the white man. The Indians had their own way, which the white men must observe if they were not to appear rude.

When talks had been agreed upon, a group of chiefs came to escort Nicollet to the nearby village. John Frémont, as his assistant, accompanied him.

The talks were held in a large tepee. Buffalo robes had been spread on the floor. A small fire burned near the doorway, and opposite the door opening sat the chief, dressed for the occasion in his finest clothing and wearing a bear-claw necklace about his neck to indicate that he was a brave man who had killed a grizzly.

Many speeches were made, with the trader interpreting for Nicollet and Frémont. Then the peace pipe was lighted and passed from man to man, each one taking a puff or so and blowing the smoke out slowly.

When the pipe came to Lieutenant Frémont, he looked at it with special interest. It was beautifully carved. The stem was made of wood, marked with a burned-in design. Eagle feathers on a strip of rawhide hung from it.

"I must get one of these pipes," the young man thought as he put it to his mouth. "The Sioux will stop carving them as soon as they find out they can buy ready-made pipes from the white men."

After this visit the men of the Topographical Engineers' Corps were free to move through Indian areas, doing the work ordered by the United States Government.

The party crossed to the east bank of the Missouri and were making camp at the convergence of a small creek, when several men, who had scouted the area by riding up onto a prominent hill, raced their horses into camp, shouting, "Buff'ler! Buff'ler!"

John dropped everything and ran to saddle his horse. Then he checked his gun, bound a large red handkerchief about his dark hair, and joined the hastily formed hunting party.

With one of the experienced men taking the lead, they proceeded as quietly and speedily as possible through the prairie, keeping hills between themselves and the grazing herd of bison.

They were ready to explode with excitement when they rode up onto a ridge and saw the moving blackness of the great beasts below them.

As the hunters urged their horses into a run with a terrific yell, the buffalo became aware of them. Heads came up. The herd turned for an instant to see what menaced them, then thundered away, dust rising like a veil from their sharp hoofs.

John Frémont rode into the midst of the buffalo with the other hunters. It was their plan to break up the stampeding animals into small groups, so that they would be easier to shoot.

In his great excitement John forgot all about plans. Immediately, he was in the midst of the running animals. He could smell them. He could hear the clashing of their short, sharp horns and their savage grunts as they dodged this way and that, confused and fearful.

A wildfire of elation swept over him. He was in the wilderness now, the real wilderness, hunting buffalo. At that moment life was almost too wonderful to endure.

After a time, during which he had never come into the right position to shoot the cow he had singled out, he dared to look around. His companions were nowhere in sight, but he rode on. His horse was keeping pace, seeming as eager as its rider.

John readied himself for a shot, but at that moment his horse faltered and seemed about to fall. John pulled up; the herd thundered past. For him, the hunt was over.

As he dismounted and stood beside his sweat-lathered horse, he felt more elated than disappointed. Some of the others had surely brought down their animals. He turned and looked back over the prairie. There was still no one in sight. He cupped his hands about his mouth and gave a long-drawn-out, "Halloo," but there was no answer.

"I'm lost," he said aloud.

There was a strange silence now after the tumult and the confusion. How far had he come? Where had the others gone? In which direction? Where was camp?

He thought it must be to the west, where the sun was slowly sinking behind low hills. He turned his horse and led him until the animal's strength returned; then he mounted and continued slowly, constantly scanning the horizon for a glimpse of a rider.

There were no paths to follow. If there had been any, they were now blotted out by the hoofs of the stampeding buffalo. At least he could follow this trail.

Gradually the sun dropped below the horizon, and darkness crept over the land. He had only his horse and the bright stars to keep him company. And, suddenly, as he looked to the stars, trying to guess his location by them, he saw a rocket streak up and explode. Relief washed over him. He was no longer lost. Camp lay to the south of west, from which point the rocket had come.

His horse was weary, and so was he. He rode a little farther, then unsaddled, watered his horse at a little stream, and went to sleep with his head on his saddle and the horse's reins tied to one of his stirrups. Carefully, before he slept, he placed his rifle with its barrel pointing in the direction of the camp.

At the first glimmer of daylight he started out again. After an hour or so he saw three riders com-

ing toward him. They saw him and waved, then
rode toward him at breakneck speed. He won-
dered what had prompted this speed, and was
more puzzled when they rode alongside and one
of them reached out in passing to slap him on the
shoulder.

When they pulled up and recovered their
breath, they told him that Nicollet had offered a
reward to the first of the trio to touch his young
assistant!

He found Nicollet and the other men ready to
begin the day's march, and after a breakfast of
buffalo meat and camp biscuits he was ready to
join them.

Summer had come. The great wilderness that
had been his goal for so long a time was unfolding
for him, mile by mile, river by river, rise by rise.
For one who loved outdoor life as John Charles
Frémont did, the work was more play than work.
He was devoted to his task. He wanted with all his
ardent young heart to help to open up this beautiful land to the millions of people who stood waiting to move into it. And each day he was learning
more and more western lore.

His teacher during this summer was Louison

Frenière, the genial Frenchman who had won Nicollet's award by being the first to touch Frémont. He and his teacher did their work, then rested and chatted until others of the expedition caught up with them.

Sometimes they lay on a grassy hillside, watching buffalo graze on the plains below. Sometimes they sat on the bank of a stream, listening to the chuckling of the moving water and the singing of meadowlarks. Sometimes they merely lay dozing while the breezes fanned them with the perfume of prairie flowers.

Often, during their day's work, Frémont and Frenière conversed in French. Sometimes they stopped to look at buffalo wallows, those shallow depressions which the big animals made in marshy places.

"You ought to see 'em," Frenière said. "They wallow like hogs, grunting and snorting as they cool themselves. Like as not the mud eases fly and mosquito bites, too."

Several times that summer they found themselves in buffalo country, and there was never any lack of meat for the party. Time and again they met friendly tribes of the Sioux Indians. At one time they were invited to camp with the tribes and

to set up their little community near the great encampment of perhaps two or three thousand Indians in their conical, skin-covered tepees.

As summer wore on and the men turned northwestward, mosquitoes began to annoy them and
their horses, making men and mounts restless. At
one lake they discovered that French Canadians
had been camped there, had been hunting and
had gone home with great loads of meat and hides
— if the deep ruts of the wagon wheels spoke truly.

Summer, with its hot days and sudden thunder-
storms, passed. The nights grew chill, and the
prairie grass turned brown. Goldenrod glowed
yellow in the lower areas, and wild asters bloomed.
Nicollet edged his party slowly homeward, stopping again at the outpost north of the Red Pipestone Quarry. The borderland trader, Joseph Renville, who had befriended them on the way to the
wilderness, received them with pleasure, and they
rested at the post for a time.

A few more excursions ended the work for the
year, and the explorers moved south. John, however, wanted one more bit of adventure.

"I'm going down river in a canoe," he told two
of his friends. "How about joining me? We can

come out at Prairie du Chien and catch a steamboat on down to St. Louis."

They agreed to join him, and for days they enjoyed the river and the life along its banks.

When they landed at Prairie du Chien, they
saw that a steamboat lay at the dock.

"Better hurry, you fellers, if you want to ride
her to Saint Looie. She's a-gettin' up steam."

John looked at his tired and grimy companions.

"How about you men?" he asked. "I feel like
resting a few days, having a hot bath and a few
good hot meals."

The others agreed.

"We'll stay with you," they said.

While they were washing for dinner, they
heard the whistle announce the departure of the
steamboat. Much later, John pushed his chair back
from the table where he had enjoyed a good home-
cooked dinner, and asked, "When does the next
boat leave?"

"That's the last one until spring," his host said.
"Storm's a-comin' in, looks like. River ices over
about this time each year."

John looked at his friends.

"Never take anything for granted," he said

with a rueful grin. "We'll have a long trip overland, boys."

The predicted storm lashed in the next morning, depositing great drifts of snow and icing the
river. There was nothing that they could do but
wait for the weather to change. It seemed forever
doing it.

The strong-willed young lieutenant learned a
lesson in caution through that experience. By the
time the skies cleared he would no doubt have
agreed that there was a lot of truth in the old saying: "Never put off until tomorrow, what you can
do today."

However, the long stay was not a total loss,
though he did worry about Nicollet's reaction to
his absence. He borrowed a pair of skates and
learned to skate on the frozen river. It was something pleasant to do while he waited.

The men bought a team and a wagon, stocked
up with provisions, and began the drive to St.
Louis. It was a long, cold journey, and they were
so glad to see the distant lights of the little city
that they shouted with glee.

John stayed only a day or so in St. Louis. Nicollet was waiting for him in Washington, where reports of the expedition were to be compiled.

4

A Stormy Romance

Soon after Lieutenant Fremont returned to Washington, he was introduced by Nicollet to Senator Thomas Hart Benton, of Missouri, whose home town was St. Louis.

Senator Benton was deeply interested in expanding the boundaries owned by the United States. Because of this interest, which he promoted wherever and whenever possible, he was eager to know what the Topographical Engineers'

Corps had accomplished during their months in the Missouri River region.

Ferdinand Hassler, who was a good friend and partner of Nicollet, had a large home on Capitol Avenue. A section of the second story was being used by the Corps as an office. One day Benton called and found Hassler, Nicollet, and John Frémont busily working on their maps and other data.

After greeting his old friends, Benton turned to John and asked to see some of his maps. John was pleased, and the two chatted amiably, finding a mutual interest in facts and figures.

Benton recognized the handsome young man's

genius in map making, and John saw in the power-
fully built, domineering Senator a man of intel-
ligence and strength.

"Young man," Senator Benton boomed, "we're
having a dinner at my home. I've invited your
chief and Mr. Hassler. Why don't you come
along?"

It had not occurred to the Senator that this
fine-looking young man would find his pretty six-
teen-year-old daughter, Jessie, irresistible, nor that
she would for a moment think of falling in love
with a second lieutenant who had no social status,
no matter how brilliant he was.

But social status meant nothing to Lieutenant
Frémont and Jessie Benton. Before they had talked
more than a few minutes, they found they had
mutual interests.

Jessie had read Schoolcraft's book, *Expedition
to the Upper Mississippi,* and they shared their
interest in the descriptions given in it and in the
beautifully done maps.

Jessie also knew of the exploring feats of some
of the famous men: Zebulon Pike, John Jacob
Astor, Jedediah Smith, Lewis and Clark, and
others who had already been brave enough to

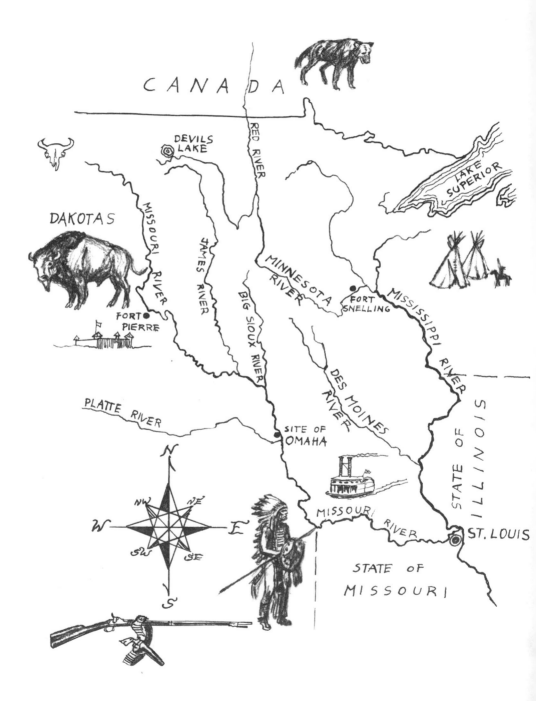

CANADA

DEVILS LAKE

RED RIVER

LAKE SUPERIOR

DAKOTAS

MISSOURI RIVER

JAMES RIVER

MINNESOTA RIVER

FORT SNELLING

MISSISSIPPI RIVER

FORT PIERRE

BIG SIOUX RIVER

DES MOINES RIVER

PLATTE RIVER

SITE OF OMAHA

STATE OF ILLINOIS

N
NW NE
W E
SW SE
S

MISSOURI RIVER

ST. LOUIS

STATE OF MISSOURI

probe the vast wilderness of the Far West.

A romance was in the making. It was not long before John decided that Jessie Benton was the girl he wanted to marry. From the first meeting, she had shown her deep interest in his work. She sympathized in his desire to climb the highest mountains and to force his way to the Pacific Ocean.

"I love to hear you talk," she told him. "Your eyes gleam and your face is aglow with eagerness. Besides, you use such poetic words! You should be writing poetry.

"And when I look at your neat and accurate maps I can almost see the covered wagons of the emigrants lurching along those trails. Perhaps you should be an artist."

"Oh, no!" John laughed. "My father was an artist. I know how little artists get for their work unless they're world famous. I lived in poverty as a child, but I don't intend to do it now."

They were strolling in the garden of the Benton home. It was early spring, and flowers were blooming. Jessie stopped and looked into John's eyes, thinking how graceful and handsome he was.

"Oh, Lieutenant Frémont! If only I were a

man! I'd like to go exploring, too."

"I'm glad you are a girl," John laughed. "And I must say the wilderness is no place for a woman at present. But someday, when the Topographical Engineers' Corps completes its surveys, you and many other women may make the trip across the desert and across the mountains in safety. One day, when I was looking down on a valley crammed full of grazing buffalo, I imagined it as it will probably be within a few years, plowed and planted, a fine stand of wheat waving in the sunshine."

Jessie looked thoughtful.

"But the poor buffalo!" she murmured. "What will happen to them?"

John Frémont shook his head somewhat dolefully.

"At the rate they're being slaughtered for their hides, I doubt whether they'll outlast the wave of progress that's on its way."

Senator Benton became very angry when he discovered the growing fondness that Jessie had for the young lieutenant. He had thought her interest only a passing fancy.

"You're too young to think of being in love, let alone getting married. I shall not invite that young man to my house again, and I want to hear no more of this affair," he stormed.

He did not realize that his daughter was as strong-willed as he was, and that she was already trying to think of a way to meet John.

John, too, was trying to find a way to talk to her, and circumstances played into his hands.

President William H. Harrison, inaugurated only the month before, had become the first President of the United States to die in office. His funeral was set for April 6, and the funeral proces-

sion would march along Capitol Avenue.

Hassler's home was on this avenue, and the office where John worked overlooked the route which the procession would take. In his determination, John did not allow the fact that he was supposed to be in that procession with other members of the Corps to worry him. Perhaps he had a cold, or perhaps the doctor he consulted had known the pangs of young love. At any rate, the doctor gave him an excuse, saying exposure on that day would be bad for his health.

With that difficulty cleared away, the tough little lieutenant, who had survived exposure to many storms, cleaned the room that overlooked the Avenue, bought flowers, teacakes, and candies, and invited the Bentons to view the colorful procession from that vantage point.

Mrs. Benton was an invalid, and Senator Benton had other duties, but Jessie accepted and came with her grandmother, who made it a point to look the other way while the lovesick couple talked beside the fireplace.

Though it might have seemed hardly the time and place for it, John told Jessie of his great love for her and asked her to marry him.

"When I met you," he told Jessie, "it was a case of love at first sight. I know I could search the world over and never find another girl who would make me the perfect wife."

Jessie was just as sure of her love for John. When they parted that day, they were engaged.

Senator Benton was enraged by the news. Mrs. Benton, who had hoped that her daughter would marry a man with money and position, was horrified. Both thought Jessie was too young to know what she was doing, and that Lieutenant Frémont, who was then twenty-eight, was wrong to have considered marriage.

"You shall not see that young man again!" Senator Benton vowed. "In his field I respect him and his genius, but he has taken advantage of my friendship. I will not sanction an engagement."

Jessie and John had no intention of breaking their engagement, although Senator Benton was used to being obeyed.

Senator Benton was a powerful political figure in the Washington of that day. He went to Joel Poinsett of the War Department and asked for his aid to get John out of the picture. Though Nicollet still needed John's help in compiling the report of the expedition, it was arranged that John should be sent on another expedition which would keep him in the wilderness for six months.

It was Nicollet, who was fond of both John and Jessie, who brought her the news.

"I am more than sad about this, Jessie," he said. "I need him. It will be a hardship to get along without him, but the order has been given. He is to survey the Des Moines River area in Iowa territory."

"You mean," Jessie cried, thoroughly shocked, "that he is to be sent into the wilderness without *you*?"

"Unfortunately, yes," Nicollet said. "I should like to go. I envy him the nights under the stars, the freedom of the plains, the joy of evenings about the campfire. That young man of yours is the best of company. He is so full of life. Everything interests him. He is forever finding rare botanical specimens and . . ."

"I know," Jessie interrupted him, her lovely eyes filled with tears and her lips trembling. "There's no one in all the world so wonderful and so exciting, but . . . ." She took a deep breath and controlled her emotion. "Oh, I *must* see him before he goes. Tell him, please. Tell him I must see him.

Somewhere. Somehow."

John Frémont was not a coward. He knew that Senator Benton had found a way to banish him for the time being, but six months was only six months. On his return to Washington, if he had his way, he and Jessie would be married.

Boldly, the night before his departure, he knocked at the Bentons' door and asked for the Senator. When Senator Benton came, glaring, to meet him, John asked with polite formality if he might tell Jessie farewell.

Senator Benton hesitated, torn between his impulse to slam the door in the face of this impetuous young man and a desire to be fair. He was stern, but not cruel, and he was actually very fond of Lieutenant Frémont.

"You may have a few minutes with her," he growled. "But there's to be no marriage for a year," he added, as Jessie came running to John, happy and sad at the same moment.

The summer months passed slowly for John, carrying out orders as patiently as possible, and Jessie, waiting for him and his small crew to return to Washington.

When he returned in October, he was so eager to see Jessie that he did not even take time to have his long hair cut before dashing off to her home.

"Oh, you look wonderful, wonderful," she cried. "You're as brown as an Indian, and being away from me has not made you thin. You look very, very well, and oh, I'm so glad you are back."

Senator Benton relaxed enough to shake hands warmly with John, but as he left the young people together, he said, "Remember! You still have six months to wait."

But another expedition was being planned. Both John and Jessie knew that this one would keep them apart for months, perhaps over a year. If they were to be married before the orders came through, they would have to act fast and without the consent of Senator Benton.

"Father will forgive me, once we're married," Jessie said. "If I didn't know that, I'd wait. Now, how will we manage?"

It took the help of several of their friends, but eventually they were pronounced man and wife.

They had been married a month before they told the Senator. He flew into a rage, as they had expected, but his anger soon faded. He gave them his blessing and asked them to spend their honeymoon at the Benton home while John made preparations to leave on the expedition. The Senator knew their time together would be short.

"Settlers are urging Congress to learn more about the land that lies beyond the Missouri River," the Senator told his new son-in-law. "They want to know what is there, and whether it is safe for them to try to make homes out there in the great 'unknown.'"

"They will have the Indians to contend with," John told him, "Indians who have lived all through the western country. A way must be found to share the land with them peacefully."

"That will come later," the Senator boomed. "The first task is to find out all about the land. To chart ways for crossing safely to the very shores of the Pacific Ocean. The unused land is a great lure. It beckons to men who ask only the chance to develop it, to make use of its fertility. We must make it ours, John!"

John knew the real aim of many of the men in high places in the Government was to win the West from Mexico before the French and English secured footholds on it.

"I take it you think the bill to appropriate money for the next expedition will soon be passed," John said.

"I expect you to be on your way by next spring," the Senator answered.

John knew the mood of the authorities. In January, 1842, John Frémont and his bride learned from President John Tyler himself that the expedition was assured.

5

On the Trail with Carson

Nicollet, the successful leader of many surveys, had not been well that winter. When the
appropriation was passed and the expedition had
been assured, he announced that he was retiring.
He named Lieutenant John Charles Frémont as
his successor.

John had proved his worth to the older man. It
was a thrill to him to have public recognition. He
began to prepare for a long and exacting trip into

the country which had been known only to trappers, guides, and a small list of daring adventurers.

Suddenly the East seemed to take a great interest in South Pass, one of the best-known "gateways" to the Oregon Country. This pass over the Continental Divide was 7,500 feet above sea level. A few emigrants had already gone over it to Oregon, among them the pioneer missionaries, Marcus Whitman and his wife, and three other missionaries who were working among the Indians in Walla Walla Valley.

Thomas "Broken Hand" Fitzpatrick, Jim Bridger, Kit Carson, and other Mountain Men had also crossed the Divide at this point at the tip of the Wind River Mountains, in south-central Wyoming.

Lieutenant Frémont and his party were to survey and map this area for the benefit of the thousands of emigrants who would soon be rushing westward. The newspapers were full of stories about the expedition. John Frémont was in the national spotlight. His name was almost a household word.

On May 1, 1842, he left Washington for St. Louis. Once more he mingled with the men of the frontier, enjoying the excitement and the colorful mixture of races and dialects. Many of his key men were to be chosen there.

A German topographer, Charles Preuss, who was skilled in describing areas of land, had gone with him from Washington. Lucien Bonaparte Maxwell, a noted hunter, was signed up at St. Louis to provide meat for the party. Basil Lajeunesse, another member of the expedition, was a man of great strength and endurance. He knew wilderness living, and he spoke some of the Indian languages. Eight men were hired to drive the carts that would carry provisions. Four oxen, sixteen mules, and a generous number of saddle horses were taken along.

Until they had boarded the steamboat that was to take them to a tiny settlement at the mouth of the Kansas River, they lacked a professional guide to see them through the wilderness and over South Pass.

But aboard the boat a small, wiry, keen-eyed man immediately attracted Lieutenant Frémont's attention. This man was Christopher "Kit" Carson.

Kit Carson was a frontiersman who had trapped and traded throughout the mountain country since he was a youngster. He had but recently come in from the wilds to visit his parents in St. Louis, but they had both died during his absence. With nothing to stay for, he was on his way west again.

He and Frémont were of about the same size, disposition, and age, Kit Carson, however, being the older by four years. Frémont knew at once that here was the man he needed to guide the expedition. Although he was paying the other men only a dollar a day and their food, he hired Carson at one hundred dollars a month. He felt he had made a wonderful bargain.

During the boat trip to the settlement, Carson told him fascinating stories about the wilderness areas — the Big Snake and the Salmon rivers, Jackson Hole, Brown's Hole, and a dozen other hidden spots that Frémont hoped to visit at some time in his journeys.

Frémont was pleased at the wealth of knowledge that Carson had stored in his brain. He also developed a sincere respect and a warm feeling of friendship for this unassuming man in the clothing of the frontier. This man knew the wilds and how to survive in them. Fear was not in him. Without an instant's hesitation, Frémont placed his faith in Carson, knowing that it would never be betrayed. Some of the strain he had previously felt began to disappear. With Carson beside him, he knew the wilderness had no problems that he could not solve.

On June 10 the group reached the mouth of the river and unloaded their equipment and supplies. Then, as the steamboat whistled its farewell, they turned their faces westward and began their dangerous journey, traveling along the bank of the Kansas.

"Just look at this beautiful land," Frémont

called to Carson later, as they rode side by side across unplowed country, soon to become a paradise for farmers. "This soil is bursting with fertility. It's crying for men to farm it."

"That's what the Injuns are afraid of," Carson said, looking a little troubled. "They can see that the white man has his eye on their country, and that their free-roaming days are about over. Can't say I blame them. This is the life they love and the land they call their own. Me! I'm a roamer, too."

"We wear the same tag," Frémont smiled.

When the party reached the ford of the Kansas, they found it raging with flood waters from a downpour that had occurred upstream. It was dangerous to try to cross it with their cartloads of priceless provisions.

Frémont had brought an India-rubber boat with him. Nicollet had had it made for emergencies such as this. Frémont had his men unpack it and spread it out on the ground beside the river — a five-foot wide, twenty-foot-long affair, reeking of the smell of its rubber coating.

When it was blown up, they loaded it with provisions, and Basil Lajeunesse, a powerful swimmer, volunteered to take the rope and pull the boat across the ford. A second man got into the boat to keep it on course.

As Basil swam out into the muddy, roaring stream, the other men pushed the loaded boat into the water. The force of the flow tore at it, turning it downstream again and again. If Lajeunesse had not been exceptionally strong, the boat would have been torn from his grasp, but he succeeded in getting it across. He then unloaded the equipment on the other side.

Some of the men swam the horses across to lead the way, and the mules and oxen followed them into the water. But the oxen floundered, finally clambering back up onto the bank on the side from which they had started.

Perhaps the men had been too sure of themselves and their ability. At any rate, when the last load was being towed, a wave caught the boat broadside and flipped it over.

Out went the steersman, followed by crates and barrels of vital supplies. The men who were watching on the bank gave a yell of dismay and jumped into the water to save whatever they could. In their excitement, some of them forgot that they could not swim, and they had to shout for help to keep from being washed downstream.

Most of the food was saved; however, the sugar was lost, as was the coffee, much to the distress of the men.

By the time the crossing had been completed, men and animals were exhausted. The horses were put out to graze; the men pitched their tents and set about cooking food for their evening meal.

Weary though he was, John Frémont enjoyed that evening on the prairie. He was a good astronomer, trained to make calculations by the stars. They were very bright that night, and the wind was still.

"What a joy to the eyes!" he said to Carson and to Preuss, as they leaned back on their bedrolls. "Away from city lights, they always seem so much brighter. They seem to dance and glow and to give off bursts of color."

Sounds took on more importance, too, on the prairie. A horse snorted. There was a rustle in the grass. John turned to see a wolf studying him, firelight in its eyes. Far off a coyote yipped. Others answered it. A bullbat swept overhead on spotted wings and flew away, calling, "Spirit! Spirit!"

The next day the expedition set off in a north-westerly direction, following a dim trail to the wide Platte River.

Soon they were deep into Indian country. They were not surprised to have a small party of Cheyennes visit their camp that night, but the Indians were peaceful and merely curious about the white men and their mission. Carson talked with them in their own language and secured valuable information about the land along the Platte and its tributary, the North Platte, which would be followed into Nebraska and Wyoming territories.

The character of the land that they crossed was ever changing. They saw rich bottom land along the Kansas and miles of curly buffalo grass like a thick carpet covering the soil. They found turbulent rivers and gentle creeks; lakes teeming with fish; flocks of prairie chickens; cranes, ducks, and other fowl. And eventually, by following the North Platte, they reached the sandhills.

This vast area was as interesting as the rest of the land, but it was different. The expedition climbed ridge after sandy ridge covered with bunch grass and soapweed. Between the ridges they saw little valleys, some of them with small, glinting lakes.

"The Indians like the sandhills," Carson told Lieutenant Frémont. "They hunt buffalo here and camp beside the lakes. Some of the tribes think the sandhills are where the dead go. They say of a dead relative, 'He has gone to the sandhills.'"

It was July by that time, and the hot sun beat down on them. But the air was sweet with the blooms of the low-growing sand-cherry bushes where bees fed, and where tall bunch grass swished its long blades as the winds blew.

In one of those little valleys they came upon a herd of buffalo. Carson, Frémont, and Maxwell hastily mounted their fastest horses and made ready for a dash into the herd. They were very close to the animals before the shaggy-maned bison saw them. A few startled grunts alerted the herd, and they were off at a run, the bulls turning now and then to see if they were still being followed.

The three hunters had raced toward the animals "like a hurricane," Frémont later wrote. When they were about to break into the herd, they gave out loud yells, and each man singled out the animal he meant to kill, then dashed in among them.

Frémont rode a trained hunting horse. It seemed as eager to get an animal as he did, and

soon Frémont was in position to shoot. The first
shot sent the cow tumbling headlong, her heart
pierced. Frémont stopped his horse and looked
around, remembering his first hunt and his experience of being lost.

Kit Carson was on the ground a short distance
away. He had tied his bridle reins to the horns of
a fat cow which he was about to cut up and pack
back to camp. Farther away, Maxwell was preparing to shoot. Frémont noticed the white smoke
curl away from Maxwell's gun barrel, and then he
saw the hunter's horse slacken its pace as Maxwell
turned to go back to the cow he had just killed.

The main herd of buffalo swept on, wild-eyed
and terrified. The hunters were content with the
three animals which they had downed. There was
feasting that night on tender buffalo hump. The
smell of the steaks, roasting over open fires, was
something to remember.

It had been difficult for young Lieutenant Frémont to leave his pretty bride, but, as she had often
reminded him, this was the most important expedition the Government had sent out since the
Lewis and Clark Expedition of 1804. His task, as

outlined by the Topographical Engineers' Corps, was "to draw a scientific and comprehensive" map of the region between St. Louis, Missouri, and South Pass.

Frémont well knew that he had not been asked to explore new territory, but only to survey and map a certain area. However, he was an explorer at heart. Once his duty was done—his orders carried out to the letter—then, if he had the time, he would feel free to wander around. He was aching to blaze a *new* trail; to strike off into the unknown, never mapped, fastnesses of the mountains that daily loomed nearer.

At Fort Laramie the party separated for a short time, Frémont taking Maxwell, Preuss, and some of the scouts with him on a side trip to the area above the South Platte, while Carson remained in charge of the main party. Preuss, however, was not feeling well, so he returned the next day to Fort Laramie.

There he found Jim Bridger with a group of trappers he had been guiding. They had just arrived from the South Pass country, where they had been attacked by a band of hostile Sioux Indians. Some of the trappers had been killed and had been

buried in the Sweetwater River area.

Bridger said that bands of Gros Ventre and Cheyenne Indians had joined the war party of Sioux and were on a rampage. He advised the Frémont Expedition to turn back, for fear they would be massacred.

Even Carson was impressed, fearless as he was. The other men were practically in a panic and in favor of abandoning their plans and returning to St. Louis. Basil Lajeunesse urged them to be calm.

When Frémont joined them on July 15, he went at once to the fort to see how much safety it afforded. The fort had been built by the American Fur Company to protect trade with the Indians, who came in two or three times a year to barter their buffalo robes and furs for blankets, calico and flannel, guns and powder, cheap novelties, and whisky.

The fort was well built, Frémont saw, with strong walls. Like most of the forts of that period, there was a tower over the entrance, with loopholes for the gun barrels of the soldiers who defended it. Unfortunately, only a few soldiers were stationed there, whereas there were thousands of Indians in the area, should they decide to attack in a body.

No more level-headed young man than Frémont ever ran an expedition. He considered every side of the serious situation at the fort before making a decision, but he was not idle. He kept the men busy surveying and mapping the fort while he visited with some of the Sioux Indians camped nearby.

The Sioux with whom Frémont conferred warned him that a war party of their young men had followed a small party of white men, intent on killing them and returning with fresh scalps at their belts. It would be well, they advised Frémont, to leave before the warriors returned, lest he and his men meet the same sad fate.

Frémont had learned through Carson, Maxwell, Lajeunesse, and others of his seasoned companions, a great deal about the Indian way of thinking. The Sioux, these men had informed him, respected a man who would confront them un-

afraid. Convinced that they were bluffing, Frémont showed no fear either of those to whom he spoke or of the absent braves with news of whom they sought to intimidate him.

"Send two or three of your young men with us," he told the delegation of chiefs that insisted upon seeing him. "Let them meet the returning war party with word that we come in peace on a mission for the Great White Father in Washington."

The chiefs said they had no young men and that they, themselves, were too old to go. It was evident that they had no intention of complying with his request.

Frémont looked very much the "chief" of his own group as he addressed them, his posture erect and his black eyes snapping.

"You say that you love the whites," he began, "then why have you already killed so many this spring? You say that you love the whites and are full of many expressions of friendship to us; but you are not willing to undergo the fatigue of a few days' ride to save our lives. We do not believe what you have said and will not listen to you. Whatever a chief among us tells his soldiers to do, is done! We are the soldiers of the great chief, your father. He has told us to come here and see this country, and all the Indians, his children. Why should we not go? Before we came, we had heard that you had killed his people, and ceased to be his children; but we came among you peaceably, holding out our hands. Now we find that the stories we heard are not lies, and that you are no longer his friends and children."

He had learned enough about the Sioux to say to them words they would understand; words with a double meaning. When he said, "We have thrown away our bodies and will not turn back," they knew he meant that come what might, he was committed to the task assigned to him, as were his men.

"When you told us that your young men would kill us, you did not know that our hearts were strong, and you did not see the rifles which my young men carry in their hands. We are few, and you are many and may kill us all; but there will be much crying in your villages, for many of your young men will stay behind, and forget to return with your warriors from the mountains. Do you think that our great chief will let his soldiers die, and forget to cover their graves? Before the snows melt again, his warriors will sweep away your villages as the fire does the prairie in the autumn.

"See! I have pulled down my white houses [the tents], and my people are ready: when the sun is ten paces higher, we shall be on the march. If you have anything to tell us you will say it soon."

The chiefs listened respectfully, their dark faces showing nothing of their feelings. Nor did they speak, although they prided themselves on their gift of oratory. Now, here was a small, young white man who dared to stand before them, his voice ringing with authority — an authority equalling their own. They liked him. They were proud of his fearlessness.

Frémont turned abruptly to Carson.

"Move them out," he ordered. Carson gave the command. The expedition began moving.

As he had expected, Frémont was suddenly approached by one of the younger chieftains.

"We are brothers," the young man said, speaking the sign language that Carson and Basil Lajeunesse understood and often used. "We will send a young man with you to meet the braves."

They kept their word. The expedition moved on. In two days they met the returning braves, who apparently had no scalps, if indeed they had fought the whites. The escorting Indian returned with the braves to Fort Laramie.

The Frémont party soon reached buffalo country. They would need meat for the winter days ahead, so they halted, built scaffolds for drying the meat, and sent out the hunters.

The high mountain flats were alive with buffalo, elk, and deer, as well as antelope. Soon the crudely made racks were covered with thin strips of meat that dried hard in the hot summer sun. Fanning winds and small fires built under the racks speeded up the drying.

The dried meat, called "jerky" by the Mountain Men, was packed in buffalo-hide bags that Frémont had bought from the Sioux. The hides had

been soaked by the Indians in wood-ash lye to remove the hair and any traces of flesh, then scraped and dried. These hides made tough, weather-tight containers and would preserve the meat indefinitely. This hide, called *parfleche*, had long been used by the Indians for storing pemmican, which was made by pounding dried meat and dried berries and then adding some fat. This was a very nutritious mixture, and could easily be carried.

As the expedition moved northwestward, they reached a section of country that looked as though a hurricane had swept through it.

"Grasshoppers!" Carson reported, riding back after scouting the trail ahead. "Let's make tracks getting through here. They've stripped the whole valley of grass and weeds. We've got to get to pasture for the animals."

They found not only good pasture farther on near the mouth of Deer Creek, but also buffalo by the hundreds grazing there. Frémont decided to cache some of the supplies. In that way their load would be lightened, and when they returned to this place, they would have food should they lose their supplies in the mountains. They marked the spot well and called it Cache Camp.

As Frémont and Carson rode along the pure mountain stream called the Sweetwater River, birds sang, and the air was filled with the pungent aroma of crushed sage. Carson entertained his companion with tales of trapping along the turbulent Big Wind River which headed in the lofty Wind River Mountains to the northwest and then joined the Little Wind River at a spot called the Double Dives.

"Fur trappers and traders had a rendezvous at the Double Dives one year," Carson recalled. "All the 'Rapahoe and Shoshone Indians in the area set up camp, and right in the middle of the jamboree a group of missionaries, including two women, rode up to make camp on the Little Wind. What with all the shootin' and hijinks, and the Injuns singing and whoopin' and dancin' they was scared most to death, afraid they'd lose their hair before the night was over."

Frémont looked at the mountains, noting their deep shadows that indicated canyons and jagged, snow-clad peaks.

"Purty, ain't they?" Carson said.

"Beautiful," Frémont agreed. "I hope I'll find time to do some mountain climbing after we've finished at South Pass."

On August 8 they reached the crest of the Continental Divide and South Pass. Though it was late summer, there were still patches of winter snow beneath the thick stands of pine.

It was evident that Indians had recently crossed there, as the tracks of their travois were fresh.

"Hunting party," said one of the men. "The way the travois poles cut into the ground shows they must have been packing good loads of meat."

When they finished surveying the area, Frémont's task was finished. As far as his official orders were concerned, he could have turned around and started home immediately. But, as always, his adventurous spirit prompted him to stay on.

A high peak — the highest, he thought, in the Wind River Range — had been his secret goal for days. So he decided to stay a few more days and climb it, if that proved possible.

Accordingly, he and his party crossed the pass and began to work up along the west side of the range, crossing the Little Sandy River, also the Big Sandy, which empties into the Green River.

In his account of this side trip, Frémont tells of

the "truly magnificent" views that continuously unfolded as he and his men climbed toward the highest reaches of the Wind River Range.

From the south end of the beautiful mountain lake that later bore Frémont's name, they gazed up at tremendous cliffs and peaks that set the explorer's blood racing through his veins. He determined to climb that high peak; to stand where no other man had stood; to plant the flag of the United States on that pinnacle of the West.

In making camp that night, he accidentally dropped his barometer. He had to spend a whole day repairing it, but he was equal to the task and was soon ready to move on. Leaving part of his men at a point where a strong fort could be built of the boulders, he and a dozen of his most reliable men, including sturdy Basil Lajeunesse, began the slow and dangerous climb up the face of the mountain he meant to conquer.

After two hours of steady climbing, they reached the first ridge of the range. While they rested, they viewed the inspiring picture below them. Cradled in the mountain's rocky side were many small lakes. Some of them were as blue as the sky; others were green or turquoise; still others were milky-white glacier lakes. About them grew green stands of lodgepole pine and shimmering-leaved, white-boled aspen.

It was an excellent place to gather botanical specimens, as Frémont immediately realized. There were many varieties of wild flowers and bushes growing in the little mountain meadows; lichen of brilliant hues clung to the granite cliffs and jumbled masses of rock. The air was keen, but filled with the perfume of pine balsam.

They camped that night beside a small stream. Frémont later recalled it with pleasure and recorded his impressions.

"The disorder of the masses which surrounded us; the little hole through which we saw the stars overhead; the dark pines where we slept; and the rocks lit up with the glow of our fires made a night picture of very rare beauty," he wrote.

The next day, after following the stream by which they had camped to its source in one of the lakes, Frémont left the animals at the camp with some of his men and, with another small group of his men, began the dangerous adventure of climbing up the steep slope on foot. He wore thin Indian moccasins. Through them he could feel the rock surfaces with his feet and so avoid slipping.

As he looked up the mountain, he had thought it only a short hike to the peak. He found, however, that distance is deceiving in thin, high air, and that strong though he was and determined to make this mountain his own, it was a tiring process.

In fact, he had expected to make the ascent and to return by dark. Instead, when the sun set and darkness threatened, the group was a long way from the top and an equally long distance from the camp below. Also, some of his men were becoming ill from the altitude, coupled with hunger and weariness.

Frémont held his position, but he sent Basil Lajeunesse back to camp with the exhausted men, telling him to return the next morning with fresh climbers.

On August 15 Frémont made the final effort to reach the peak, but almost plunged to his death with victory close at hand.

"I sprang upon the summit," he wrote in his journal, "and another step would have precipitated me into an immense snowfield, five hundred feet below."

Panting, he stood victorious on the second

highest mountain in the Wind River Range, 13,750 feet above sea level. The hot summer sun beat down on his slouch hat, and at the same time the snow bit through the thin soles of his moccasins. During the labor of the climb, he had opened his blue flannel shirt at the throat, and now that he had reached the pinnacle, he realized what a great amount of energy the climb had required.

His black eyes surveyed the scene. A more magnificent panorama could hardly be imagined. Below the climbers the mountain unfolded, ridge by ridge, to the sage-clad flats. Beyond them, the three Tetons towered, snowy and immense.

It was a solemn moment and one of supreme satisfaction to the brilliant young explorer.

The solemnity did not last long. From somewhere a bumblebee winged in to buzz inquisitively around him. The men who had followed him to the peak laughed. The spell was broken.

"Unfurl the flag," Lieutenant Frémont ordered.

When this was done, he tied the bright symbol to a ramrod and placed it firmly where, as he later wrote, "never a flag waved before."

Then the men began the dangerous descent. They found the men who had remained below re-

vived after a good night's rest and plenty of nour-
ishing food. The horses and mules had eaten their
fill of green grass. The men rested together at camp
that night and rejoined those at the main camp
next day.

On the return trip to St. Louis, according to
Lieutenant Frémont's orders, the party was to survey the upper regions of the Platte River. They
reached that stream on August 24.

This, the men decided, would be a good place
to put the rubber boat into action again. They
launched it and had started downstream when
Frémont realized that this feat might well prove to
be the most dangerous task he had ever under-
taken. The North Platte was a treacherous stream,

winding through narrow, steep-sided canyons and over fields of sharp rocks. But dangerous though it might be to ride the frail craft through the canyons, with their roaring rapids, it would also be a terrific task to carry the boat and the provisions through the rough areas that bordered the stream.

They were congratulating themselves that they had ridden safely through some of the rapids when they came to a long canyon with perpendicular walls, at least five hundred feet high in spots. This time luck failed them. The boat was ripped and overturned. Two of the men narrowly escaped drowning, and some of the instruments and technical notes went downstream, never to be recovered.

The party was footsore and weary when, finally, they reached Cache Camp. It was heartening, though, to find all their stored provisions just where they had left them.

It was the last day of August when they reached Fort Laramie. They rested three days, then started out on the easy and last phase of the journey.

The boat which Frémont had ordered before leaving on the expedition, was waiting for them on the Missouri River. They went aboard it on October 1. It had taken a full month to cross the prairie lands.

As Lieutenant-Frémont watched the land recede as the steamboat headed away from the tiny dock, he felt a sudden pang of sorrow. Already he was missing the feel of the curly buffalo grass beneath his moccasined feet. Also, he knew there would be moments when, as he bent over his desk, he would remember the stimulating odor of sage, the chuckle of a mountain stream, the call of night birds in the afterglow of a sunset on the plains.

He turned away to look forward. Jessie would be waiting for him, and that was wonder and joy enough for the present.

6

A National Hero

Lieutenant John Frémont's success as an explorer made him a national hero overnight. Stories about him and his scaling of Mt. Frémont in the vastness of far-away Wyoming made headlines in the foremost newspapers of the day. The report he gave to the Topographical Engineers' Corps was published by the Government in the spring of 1843, and thousands of copies were sold. Everyone wanted to learn about the Far West and the possibilities of seeking a home there.

John's career had been launched at a very fortunate time. His expeditions and his vivid accounts of his journeys appealed to multitudes.

Those who knew him well honored him for his expert and accurate surveying. They likewise respected him for his appreciation of the aims of the men who knew that the West must be opened. Expanding ideas and plans made an expansion of land necessary.

The newspapers were correct in predicting that Frémont's favorable reports would start a great wave of immigration westward. The public response to the 1842 expedition was so gratifying to Congress that it immediately appropriated money for another one, with Lieutenant John Charles Frémont to head it.

This suddenly famous young man had now become a father. On the same night he returned from the South Pass Expedition, Mrs. Frémont gave birth to a daughter, whom they named Lily.

When the Frémonts received orders for the second expedition, they decided to move to St. Louis, since the arrangements for this expedition would necessarily be made in that city. This arrangement would also allow Lieutenant Frémont to spend more time with his wife and baby Lily.

The trip from Washington was a trip many families would try to avoid, if possible. Senator and Mrs. Benton; the Frémonts, their baby and its nurse; the three Benton children — Randolph, who had accompanied his brother-in-law on the expedition as far as Fort Laramie, and the two young girls — made up the party.

The group traveled from the capital to Baltimore by train; from there to Philadelphia by steamboat; from there to Harrisburg, Pennsylvania, by a horse-drawn mail coach; from there by canal boat to Pittsburgh, Pennsylvania; and finally, by steamboat to their destination. The entire journey was of about two weeks' duration.

Lieutenant Frémont and his wife and her father enjoyed the trip very much, since it gave them an opportunity to talk with many people and to learn their views. They found everyone interested in the opening of the West. It seemed as if the entire population of the East was slowly shifting westward.

Senator Benton's old home dated back to the early days of St. Louis and to his own youth. When he bought the acreage on which he later built his large and comfortable home, it was in the country.

But the city of St. Louis in those boom days had spread out until the old home was no longer isolated.

St. Louis at that time was an exciting, colorful embarkation point, and the Mississippi River was the frontier. At the docks on sailing days, one could see many families from the East preparing to stake their lives and their futures on the Great Plains. Traders and trappers and Indians and restless men of all races mingled, and around them was an air of intense anticipation, which was shared to the full by the Frémonts and Senator Benton.

Everyone in St. Louis had heard about Lieutenant Frémont. In the minds of many he was pictured standing on Frémont Peak, as it was to be known later, the Stars and Stripes in his hand. Both young and old sought out the Frémonts. Had they accepted all the invitations they received, they would have had no time to themselves. Though Lieutenant Frémont was a lithe and graceful dancer and enjoyed social affairs after his long stay in the wilds, he had work to do, so he had little time for dancing.

Every day he kept busy hiring men and securing provisions for the long journey ahead. This time his first objective was the Great Salt Lake in Utah, and his orders from the Topographical Engineers' Corps were to connect his 1842 Expedition with the survey which Captain Charles Wilkes had made on the Pacific Coast.

Captain Wilkes, commanding a fleet of four small ships, had sailed into San Francisco Bay in October, 1841, after charting some islands of the Pacific and certain unexplored arctic and antarctic ice fields.

He was a stern and sour person. The light-hearted Californios then living in a little town called Yerba Buena, later to take the name San Francisco, angered him. He disliked their dancing and feasting and refused all invitations to join them. In fact, he hated California as a whole. He

wrote to the Navy Department, saying the land was without either fertility or beauty.

However, since he had been ordered to do so, he sent a young Navy lieutenant, George Foster Emmons, with a small surveying party, from the mouth of the Columbia River, along the Willamette River, to the Sacramento Valley and Sutter's Fort.

This was the survey with which Frémont was to connect. He had read about it, and about how John Sutter, dressed in the uniform of a Mexican army officer, had greeted the Navy men. At that time Frémont had no idea that gold, discovered at Sutter's mining site, would cause a stampede of gold seekers in 1849 — only six years hence.

He knew the feeling of Government officials about the country called California. He knew they feared England, France, or Russia would attempt

to wrest it from Mexico unless the United States made some successful play for it.

He was well aware of the part he might play in this game of national chance. If, through his scientific expedition, he was able to talk with the Americans who lived in California, as well as to some of the Californios who did not like Mexican rule, he might be able to learn how the United States could come into possession of California.

Perhaps he may have had a possible clash in mind when he asked Colonel Stephen Watts Kearny, a close friend of the Bentons, if he might take along a small cannon. His excuse for wanting it was that it might protect his large exploring party from attack by hostile Indians which they were almost certain to meet.

This 1843 Expedition, as it was to be known, was to cover a much larger area than the previous one. Frémont was asked to find a pass in the Rockies, one that was easier to climb than South Pass. He was to inspect Great Salt Lake and the Great Basin, then connect with the Wilkes Exploration on the Columbia River and locate a pass in the Sierra Nevadas. It was a very large order and one that would no doubt keep him away from home for a long time.

Frémont had not been able to get in touch with Kit Carson, but he did have with him the famed guide and mountaineer, Thomas Fitzpatrick, who had been given the name "Broken Hand" by the Indians, because he had lost three fingers on one hand in a frontier accident. Fitzpatrick was one of the best guides in the West, equal, many thought, to Kit Carson.

The party left St. Louis as scheduled and proceeded over the now familiar trail to Bent's Fort on the Arkansas River, where Frémont hoped he might meet Carson, or at least have word from him.

"Is Kit Carson here?" he asked the trader who came out to greet the Frémont party on its arrival at the fort.

"Nope! Last I heard, he was off to Taos on some sort of mission," replied the trader.

Disappointed, Frémont moved his party forward, but about three days later he spotted a lone rider racing toward them. There was something familiar about the way the man sat his horse. It was — it had to be — Carson!

Frémont turned his horse and rode to meet his good friend.

They slid from their saddles in a cloud of dust and rushed to clasp hands.

"What do you mean, running off without me?" Carson shouted.

"Just didn't think I'd need you this time," Frémont countered. "Of course, if you want to come along..."

Both men knew the depth of the other's affection. Laughingly they mounted their horses again and joined the party, where Carson was welcomed heartily.

That night they sat around the campfire for a long time, discussing with the other men plans for conquering the wilderness.

Frémont was now free to explore some of the mountain regions of Colorado. He was scouting for the easy gateway in the Rockies, through which the many westbound families might drive their oxen hitched to tall Conestoga wagons.

They worked up along the eastern slope of the Rockies, seeing many possible routes, but no gateways. These lofty mountains reared their heads from 10,000 to 14,000 feet above sea level, and there were at least a hundred majestic peaks. The passes would no doubt, Frémont guessed, be lofty, too. For the time being he and his men merely scouted the area, without trying to force a way over the great barrier.

Continuing northward, they again reached the old Oregon Trail and crossed the Divide at South Pass. Fitzpatrick, who had spent much time in that area, told the men that nuggets of gold had been found in the streams on the Divide. None of them realized, however, that one day South Pass City would come into being, where thousands of gold seekers would mine and pan the streams for gold.

They left South Pass and continued to Bear River, following it south. Trappers had reported that it emptied into the Great Salt Lake, which was Frémont's first objective.

It was already early September when they came to a high point from which they could see the immense body of salt water glinting and gleaming in the ruddy evening light, and they glimpsed the great valley where a city would soon begin to rise.

"It's like an inland sea!" Frémont exclaimed. "I see several large islands, but I can't tell from here whether they are wooded or not. We'll have to paddle over in the rubber boat and find out for ourselves."

For this work he would not need all his men. A small group would be enough to do all that would be required. So he selected the geologist, Preuss; Carson, the guide; Basil Lajeunesse, who could be depended upon for loyalty, strength, and endurance; a fourth man, Jean Baptiste Bernier, and three others, who would maintain the camp and assist the main party if needed.

The remainder of the large group went north to Fort Hall, about one hundred miles away, under the leadership of Fitzpatrick, and waited for Frémont's party there.

Fitzpatrick was to get supplies for the trip into Oregon and see that the animals were rested and fed.

That first evening there was a brilliant sunset, and after that a quiet twilight. While frogs croaked in a chorus, the men talked about the next day's work and what it might disclose. They had heard tales of a terrible whirlpool in the middle of the Great Salt Lake, and they had no desire to be sucked down into it, if the tales were true. And they were also concerned about their boat. It had done well in the rapids of the North Platte, until it was cut by the rocks. Would it be equal to the waves in this lake?

At dawn the next morning they arose and examined the fragile craft. It had been repaired, but not very well. They suddenly began to realize how serious it would be for them if it should begin to leak when they were too far out on the lake to swim back.

Since the weather was mild and there was no wind to whip up the waves, the situation seemed favorable, however.

Then, as they began to inflate the boat, Carson discovered leaks in two of the air cylinders.

"If this boat is to stay afloat," he said, "one man will have to work the bellows all the time and keep these cylinders filled with air."

In spite of the leaks, they loaded the provisions they would need, took their blankets, the instruments which Frémont and Preuss required, and fifteen gallons of fresh water. Then they put the boat into the river and floated down toward the lake, enjoying the day and shooting enough ducks for their supper.

That night they camped at a spot where the river sand made a small delta. The next morning they waded into the soft mud, pushing and pulling their boat, while flocks of little water birds flew up from the reeds and mud, crying in protest.

The men dragged the boat in mud for about a mile before the water began to deepen. Then, suddenly, they came to a ridge of black rock. Beyond this ridge the water was salty, and there was sand beneath their feet. They pushed the boat over this boundary ridge and scrambled into it, ready for the adventure to begin.

The day was still calm, but getting uncomfortably warm. As they rowed, they noticed that the water deepened, becoming very clear and a bright green color. They also noticed that spray from the paddles was drying into a crust of salt on their skin and clothing.

Nevertheless, they were in a happy mood until they discovered that they could no longer touch lake bottom with the tips of their paddles.

"Cap'n," said Carson suddenly, "what's that yonder?" He pointed to some white objects that had appeared near one of the islands. "Would you take a look through the glass, and see?"

The men stopped paddling, and Fremont scanned the white objects.

"Whitecaps," he reported. "Looks as though there's a strong breeze coming up the lake."

The adventure by this time had taken a serious turn. The men fell silent. Real concern showed in their faces when the divisions between the air cylinders gave way. The bellows had to be worked continuously.

They made slow progress after the wind whipped up and the waves began to slap the boat. Gradually, by moving into the lee of the island they meant to explore, they came into smoother water. About noon they found a place where they could climb the salt-whitened cliffs, and they went ashore, carrying their surveying instruments and provisions.

These were the first white men, and possibly

the first men of any race, to set foot on one of the islands of the Great Salt Lake. In one way their visit was a disappointment. They had hoped to find trees and streams and a variety of wild life on the island, but it had none of these features. They saw no animals of any kind on the island, no trees, no water. While they were eating their supper a magpie flew in, peered at them, squawked, and flew away again.

That night they went to sleep in perfect security. No one was there besides themselves; no one would be likely to come. However, in the night, they awoke to find that the wind had risen to near gale proportions, and that a surf was booming against the cliffs. The force of it made the island shake beneath them.

In the morning the lake was dark and forbidding. The wind was still blowing, but with less force. The exploring party ate hastily and made ready to return to the base camp.

"Think we'll make it?" one of the men asked.

"Of course!" was Frémont's answer, but there was nothing light and jesting in his manner.

They had trouble making headway against the wind and had to fight to keep the boat from being blown out into the open parts of the great lake.

Frémont was making depth soundings now and then, and in order to do this, he asked the men to stop paddling. Each time, they lost ground. Finally, when the soundings showed only one fathom, the men gave a cheer and began to paddle with renewed vigor, eager to reach the safety of the other shore.

They took ashore a bucketful of salt water, which they boiled down that evening. The crust of salt that resulted was carefully packed away for seasoning their food.

By the time they started back north along the Bear River, they were short of provisions, but they made the trip to Fort Hall without trouble and found their companions waiting for them, with provisions ready for the next lap of the journey.

The lateness of the year, combined with the fresh snow on the mountains, had convinced Frémont that he should proceed with the exploration with haste, leaving complete exploration of Great Salt Lake for some future time. It seemed advisable to reach a milder climate as speedily as possible.

7

"Sutter's Fort's Ahead!"

THE EXPLORERS were following the Oregon Trail along the south bank of the Snake River when a heavy snowfall overtook them. The main party went into camp immediately, but Frémont turned back to Fort Hall to buy additional provisions, as well as more horses and oxen.

He had no illusions about the remainder of this trip to the Oregon Territory. It was not going to be a pleasant outing.

However, in spite of miserable weather, both cold and wet, he pushed on. On September 27 he divided his party again, leaving part of the men and the heavy equipment — including the clumsy and, so far, useless cannon — with Fitzpatrick. He took Carson, a few other men, and the light equipment with him and started on toward the Fishing Falls.

Friendly Indians and the pleasure of fishing for salmon greeted them at the falls. The Indians brought fish, offering these for clothing, which they needed very badly, since some of the men wore nothing but a shirt in the freezing cold. Frémont's men, however sympathetic they were, could not give up any of their own clothing.

By October 13 Frémont and his small party had reached the great Western Slope, of which the Senators in Washington had heard so much. Already they found the climate less severe, and they left the beaten trail into Oregon to explore and chart a direct route through the Blue Mountains. On October 24 they reached the settlement in the Walla Walla Valley that had been started by the pioneer missionary, Marcus Whitman.

Another day's ride brought them to the Colum-

bia River, and from there Frémont went on by boat
to Fort Vancouver at the mouth of the great river.

He had completed another of the objectives of
the expedition. He had reached the same spot from
which Lieutenant Emmons had begun his southward march along the Willamette River. He had
also connected with the Wilkes Expedition route.

At Fort Vancouver he purchased more supplies, and then returned to his men on November
18.

The party was together now, the group under
Fitzpatrick having arrived, as planned, at The
Dalles, on the Columbia River.

Frémont found it difficult to feed such a large
party, so he sent several of the men home. He also
left most of his heavy wagons behind, but took
along the heavy howitzer that had been lent to him
by Colonel Kearny.

When he turned south from The Dalles, following the course of the Deschutes River, he had
with him twenty-five men and enough provisions
for three months.

He soon found that this route was a rough one.
It was bordered on the west by the Cascade Mountains, whose beautiful conical peaks revealed their

volcanic past. From them, no doubt, had spewed the ridges and jumbles of broken lava that made travel over them so slow and so dangerous.

There was no danger of getting lost, however, for both Carson and Fitzpatrick had been over that country.

Frémont's worst worry, at that time, was the fact that his wife might think him lost, since he had not been able to get word to her. Neither she nor the Topographical Engineers' Corps knew at which point he intended to enter California, and the Corps would not be able to send help, even if it were needed.

The men began to feel the bitter cold before they reached Klamath Lake early in December, and by then snow was falling. The days were extremely cold. Pack animals slipped and slid on the icy rocks, more often they fell. Their packs then had to be removed before the animals could get back on to their feet.

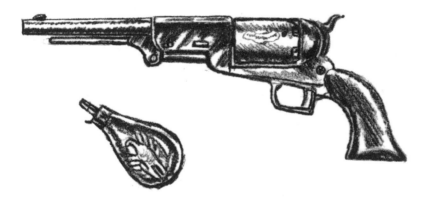

Until they reached the Klamath Lake area, the men had no trouble with Indians. But one night in their camp at that place, they were alerted by the snorting of their horses, and they saw a band of Indians on a ridge not far away.

"Fire the cannon!" Frémont ordered. "That will scare them away. I have no desire to kill them unless they insist on making it a real fight."

The Indians charged toward them, but were turned back by the noise and smoke of the cannon, and they disappeared as if by magic. This turned out to be the first and last time the howitzer was brought into action.

The explorers worked eastward from Klamath Lake, finding the way increasingly tiring and the cold weather unbearable. Food supplies began to run low. Rations had to be made smaller, and still smaller. The hours of travel were also decreased, because of the exhaustion of the men and the animals. A Klamath Indian, who had been scouting for them for several days, refused to go any farther.

The deep snow had melted during one warm day, then had frozen over during the night. The crust that resulted was like glass. Both men and horses suffered cuts on their legs as they plodded through it, breaking trail. But in spite of Frémont's innate poetic streak, he was not a soft man. He was tough-minded and he was determined not to be defeated, either by the weather or the roughness of the land.

It was on December 16 that a welcome sight greeted them. They had climbed a steep ridge to see below them a beautiful blue lake surrounded by green prairie land. They could hardly believe their eyes.

"It's almost too good to be true," Frémont said. "But it is true. The problem is how to get down to it."

Patience was required to find safe footing down to this hidden paradise. It was worth the struggle, however, and they hastily made camp and turned the hungry animals out on the green pasture.

"We'll call it Summer Lake," Frémont said, and it is known by that name today.

The water was pure and good there, but the next small lake was a disappointment. The water was not fit to drink. The expedition named that lake Abert, for the head of the Topographical Engineers' Corps, Colonel John J. Abert. The third lake, reached on Christmas Day, was named in honor of the holiday.

Soon after Christmas, and as they were working their way slowly southward through the north-western part of Nevada, another storm blew in with high winds that made travel doubly danger-ous.

They had not previously met any Indians in that district, and so were as surprised as the little band of half-starved and almost nude Indians they came upon in the storm. The Indians had been huddled together in a sagebrush shelter, but they scattered and ran to hide in the rocks when the white men appeared.

"They've probably never seen a white man before," Frémont said. "They may think we are ghosts."

Before long, they began to see many other signs of Indian occupation. On several occasions they discovered that a mule or a horse had been stolen at night, probably to be slain for food.

On December 29 they came to a well-marked, recently used Indian trail. They traveled along it for several miles, hoping that it would lead up and over the Sierras which loomed to the west. But this proved to be a false hope, and New Year's Day, 1844, found them in a dense fog that made travel impossible. They could not break camp for three long days.

But the worst was yet to come. Their horses and mules, unable to find anything to eat, began to die of starvation. Optimist though he was, Frémont looked worried when the fifteenth one dropped dead in the snow.

When the fog lifted, the spirits of the men also became lighter. Food for the horses was found, and on January 10 they saw not far to the south of them a long lake, where a great stone, shaped like a pyramid, jutted up from its center. They called this place Pyramid Lake. While they encamped on its banks, they ate the last of the cattle they had brought down from the Columbia River, and so were strengthened for the next phase of the adventure.

At the south end of this lake they found Indians fishing for salmon trout in the river which flowed into it from the Sierras. These Indians looked well fed and cheerful — a much better type than those they had found huddling in the sagebrush farther north. The Indians brought a liberal gift of fish for the evening meal, but Frémont, knowing that they might take extra payment in horses or mules, set up a guard that night.

When the men looked up at the massive wall of the Sierra Nevada Mountains, along the eastern slopes of which they were working, they believed it would be impossible for either men or animals to find a way to cross them. But this was Frémont's aim: to find a good pass for westbound travelers.

"I've been over there, in the Sacramento Valley," Carson declared, squinting up at the forbidding whiteness of the cliffs and steep slopes. "Soon's I get on top of one of those peaks, I'll know where I am. It's been fifteen years, but I'll never forget my landmark. It's a little mountain across the Bay, called Monte del Diablo — Devil Mountain."

The men were in a state of suspense. The supreme effort was about to be made. They would find a way over the mountains and reach Sutter's Fort in the Sacramento Valley, or they would probably perish trying to do so.

Frémont refused to think of failure. "I must succeed," he told himself. "Whatever it costs me, I must master these mountains."

"Hurts me all over to think how nice and warm it is over in the valley on the other side," Carson sighed, scratching his head. "Think of it. No snow. Gentle, warm rains. Grass for the critters. Flowers, green hills . . ."

"Stop talkin' and get us there," one of the men growled.

In actual miles it was not a long journey, but that was little consolation to the men who had to scale those heights through snow and ice.

By this time the party was reduced to living on pine nuts. Indians survived on these nuts, so Frémont's men felt certain they could, too. They still had their guns and ammunition, and occasionally they shot a deer or an elk. If they had no other choice but to starve, they would eat their oxen, horses and mules.

When the sun broke through the clouds on the morning of February 2, the party hastily broke camp and began the climb. After a struggle that left them all weak and panting, they reached a ledge which served as their campsite for the night.

The next day Frémont called Carson aside.

"It has to be done," he said. "Today!"

"We'll do it," Carson promised.

The two men left Fitzpatrick and the rest of the party at the campsite and challenged the mountains. Step by step, they strained for toeholds and handholds; numbed by the bitter cold they struggled up onto one of the higher peaks.

Carson took a deep breath.

"There she is!", he pointed. "See? There's my little mountain. Sutter's Fort's dead ahead."

That valley looked near, but it would mean days of hard work in the bitter cold to move the men over the crest and down the other side.

It took the party fifteen days to reach the top of the pass. When they made camp at the summit, 9,338 feet above sea level, the date was February 20.

The descent to the valley was almost as perilous as the ascent to the crest. They had to cut paths through the snow with axes; they crawled on hands and knees over snowfields so icy that they could not keep their footing; every day was an agony of work. Yet every day's move forward was a triumph, and no one faltered.

One day, as he attempted to jump a mountain torrent, Frémont slipped and fell in. Carson, thinking his friend had been injured, jumped in after him. Frémont was not hurt, and the two emerged, dripping wet and shivering, but laughing at the spectacle they must have made for the rest of the party.

A mule, carrying a load of valuable botanical specimens collected by Frémont, lost its footing and plunged down a precipice. The cannon which they had brought 2,000 miles at a terrific cost in mule power, slid into a canyon, never to be recovered. Other pieces of valuable equipment were lost, but at last the tall pines began to give way to live oaks and bushy growth. The worst was over.

Lieutenant Frémont and Kit Carson mounted their best saddle horses and rode ahead to Sutter's Fort, where they hastily bought food and other comforts for the men still back on the trail.

Later Frémont said, "A more forlorn and pitiable sight than they presented cannot be imagined. They were all on foot, each man weak and emaciated, leading a horse or a mule."

Of the large herd of animals they had driven southward from the Columbia, only thirty-three survived to reach the green grass of the Sacramento Valley.

The party had no sooner reached Sutter's Fort than Frémont began to plan the trip home. He knew they had probably been given up as lost, and he was anxious about his wife and baby.

The other men, after a few days' rest and plenty

of good food, were as eager as he was to start home. All of them were in the best of spirits and health when they left Sutter's Fort on March 24. As they looked back on the problems they had encountered, they knew they were lucky to have lived through the experience.

Lieutenant Frémont had purchased the best supplies available for their homeward journey, and they were also taking with them thirty head of cattle, as well as one hundred-thirty horses and mules.

How different from the mountain crossing was this trip along the San Joaquin Valley! Fields of golden California poppies intermingled with the bright blue of lupine. The hills were knee-high in wild oats, the roadway bright with yellow mustard, monkey flower, owl's clover, and a dozen other varieties of floral beauty. Frémont gathered many specimens of the flowers to show to his sponsors in the East.

"I'm convinced," he told Carson, "that California should be under the flag of the United States. The Californios I have talked with seem eager to have a change from bungling Mexican rule. I'm sure it will be a part of the United States in the near future."

After experiencing the rigors of the Sierras, crossing the Tehachapi Mountains was easy for both men and horses. But now they faced the heat of the desert instead of the cold of the mountains.

When they reached the Old Spanish Trail, they turned northeastward, traveling slowly during the night to escape the fiery rays of the sun during the day. One day they had no water. This situation was as bad as breaking trail through ice and snow. It was when the thirsty stock began to forge eagerly ahead that they knew water was not far away.

Before many more days had passed, they reached the Virgin River and began to travel with the Great Basin of the Salt Lake in sight. This time they were not going to explore the region. Their immediate task was to find a pass through the Rocky Mountains.

Fortunately, Joseph Reddeford Walker, another great scout of pioneer days, heard of their presence in that area. He left the party with which he had been traveling and joined Frémont's group. He had been through the territory they were about to enter, and he was willing to share his knowledge with them.

Even with his help, it was July 1 before they

arrived at Bent's Fort, where the expedition was to break up. William Bent fired the cannon as a welcome. Kit Carson hurried on to Taos and his family; Walker stayed on at Bent's Fort, as did some of the other men.

Frémont and the rest of his men lost no time in striking out across the now familiar Indian country. They were bound for the Missouri River and a steamboat ride to St. Louis.

8

Another Honor Conferred

By MANY PEOPLE, including the Topographical Engineers' Corps, the Frémont Expedition to California had been given up as lost. Frémont's wife, however, believed in the endurance of her husband and was anxiously awaiting his return.

When he did arrive, she was overjoyed, but her happiness was a trifle marred by information she had concealed from him on his departure. She lost no time in confessing what she had done.

"John," she said. "I kept an order from you. I hope you'll forgive me."

"An order?" he asked. "From whom?"

"From Colonel Abert. He ordered you to return. You were at Kaw's Landing, just ready to start west. He was angry about your taking the cannon."

"But I had permission from Kearny," Frémont said, puzzled. "And if I returned, who was to head the party?"

Mrs. Frémont's eyes filled with tears.

"He was going to send someone to relieve you of command," she said. "And, oh, John, I couldn't let that happen. That's why I sent you the message to start at once."

Frémont paced the floor, wondering whether this matter would react unfavorably on the results of his hard work. Finally he relaxed and smiled at Jessie.

"When they see my reports," he said, "I think they'll forgive us the cannon incident."

"You did bring it back with you, didn't you?" his wife asked.

Frémont shook his head.

"The Sierra snows stole it from us," he said, his

face grim as he thought of the days he had strained and starved in the mountains. "It's up there, in a canyon. We're lucky we're not buried there with it."

He was right about the officials' opinion of his reports. When they read his account of the expedition, they were delighted with his work. Nothing was said about the cannon.

Congress printed the reports by the thousands, and these sold like wildfire, just as the first ones had done. Teachers even read them to the children in the schoolrooms.

Lieutenant Frémont and California became known throughout the Union.

One day an official invitation was received by the Frémonts.

"We've been invited by James Knox Polk to a reception," Mrs. Frémont cried. "That's proof he approves of your work, and you know he'll be inaugurated president next March!"

"We'll go," agreed Frémont. "My guess is that he'll ask Congress to order another expedition."

President-elect Polk greeted the Frémonts warmly, then drew them into another room, where a group of Government officials waited to discuss

California with the pathfinder.

"Geographically," one of the officials said, "California belongs to us. The entire Pacific Coast, for that matter, also does. Should other nations claim part of that seacoast, there could be never-ending disputes."

"That's right," the others agreed. "The problem is: How can we come into possession of California without war with Mexico?"

No one wanted to suggest an answer, but it was easy to see that everyone was in favor of another expedition into California. Soon after the March inauguration of President Polk, Congress voted fifty thousand dollars to finance Frémont's third expedition.

One day a tall, soldierly gentleman in uniform called on the Frémonts. He was General Winfield Scott. He had a mission.

"You have won many honors, Lieutenant Frémont," he said, "both at home and abroad. It is my pleasure to confer yet another on you."

The official document which he gave to Frémont conferred on the young lieutenant the rank of captain, and it read: "For gallant and meritorious services in the two expeditions headed by himself."

When General Scott left the Frémonts, Mrs. Frémont turned to her husband.

"What is the first thing you're going to do, *Captain* Frémont?"

"The first thing? Why, I'm going to ask you to get a letter off immediately to Kit Carson. Remind him that he promised to go with me if a third expedition were ordered," Frémont told her.

The letter was written and dispatched by an express messenger. When the rider reached Taos, New Mexico, he discovered that Carson had bought land, and, in partnership with another mountaineer, Richard Owens, had planted a crop.

Carson's plans for living a quiet life vanished

when he read the letter. He could not resist the thrill of exploring again with his good friend as leader.

"Let's sell out and join him," he suggested.

"What're we waitin' for?" grinned Owens.

"Tell Frémont we'll meet him at Bent's Fort," Carson told the rider.

Sixty-two men, including Carson, Owens, Maxwell, and Walker, the guides, and six keen-eyed, steel-nerved Delaware Indians devoted to Captain Frémont, made up the Third Expedition. All of them were well-armed — a necessity in territory where Indian attacks were almost daily occurrences.

Moving fast, Captain Frémont and his men explored the upper reaches of the Arkansas River and the land around Utah Lake, then spent a week at Salt Lake, thoroughly charting it. Toward the end of October they moved on into Nevada and to the headwaters of the Humboldt River, so named by Frémont to honor Baron Friedrich Heinrich Alexander von Humboldt, a noted scientist, traveler, and botanist, whose work the captain had long admired.

At that point Frémont sent Walker and the greater portion of the party on to Walker's Lake, on the east side of the Sierras.

"The rest of us will survey this northern portion of Nevada and meet you at the lake," he said.

They met at the lake only to divide again, Walker taking the main party south along the Sierras to Walker Pass, and Frémont, Carson, and a few others crossing the Sierra in the Lake Tahoe region.

The presence of a large party of armed men, led by a captain of the United States Army, was disturbing to the Mexican authorities. Governor Juan Bautista Alvarado sent a messenger to ask them what they were doing in Mexican Territory.

"I am in command of a scientific expedition," Frémont told the messenger politely. "I shall be proceeding toward Oregon."

Governor Alvarado gave Frémont and his men permission to spend the winter in California, provided they stayed away from the coast. At that time Frémont was encamped near the little village of San Juan, built up around the twenty-first and largest of the California missions—Mission San Juan Bautista. This mission was only about ten miles from the ocean.

In March the welcome of the Mexican governor wore thin and he sent word by General José Castro that Frémont and his men were to leave California at once.

At first, Frémont refused to leave because of Governor Alvarado's permission. Later he relented and moved slowly up the Sacramento River to the Klamath Lake region, across the California line in Oregon.

He had no idea, until later, that the President of the United States had sent Archibald H. Gillespie, a Marine Corps lieutenant, to California, with a verbal and highly confidential message for him.

Gillespie arrived in Monterey, delivered the message to Thomas O. Larkin, the United States Consul, then secured a horse and raced after Frémont.

What Gillespie told Captain Frémont has never been made public. Frémont's friends were later convinced that Gillespie had relayed a message from high authority to the effect that California would be welcomed into the Union if a transfer could be made peacefully.

This fact would explain Frémont's immediate move southward, back into California, where mighty events were taking shape.

Until then, Captain Frémont had fully intended to be back home by September. He had no idea that he was about to be plunged into a short, but bitter, period of argument and war.

Many Americans had drifted into the Mexican territory of California. They wanted California for the United States, and some of them were so willing to fight for it that they staged the "Bear Flag" Revolt and appealed to Captain Frémont, as a representative of the United States, to protect them from a fancied attack at Sonoma.

Captain Frémont moved swiftly from his camp at the junction of the Bear and Feather rivers, reaching Sonoma on the Fourth of July. The Americans asked him to command their forces, and, as a result, the Stars and Stripes were hoisted at that place on July 9.

Though they did not know it that day, the flag had already been flown over the Custom House in

Monterey on July 7, by Commodore John Drake
Sloat. He had sailed into the harbor on July 2,
aboard the *Savannah*. On July 7 he landed a
naval force, issued a proclamation stating that the
United States was at war with Mexico, and that he
intended to take immediate possession of California.

By his order, Captain John B. Montgomery,
aboard the U.S.S. *Portsmouth* at Yerba Buena,
also hoisted the Stars and Stripes.

Commodore Robert F. Stockton, who succeeded Sloat within a few days, held a conference
with Captain Frémont.

"I'm in charge of United States forces here," he

said, "and I want you to stay here as head of the California Battalion, as your men and other Americans willing to join your expeditionary group will be called."

They sailed with him to San Diego and marched overland to Los Angeles, certain they would have to fight it out with the Mexicans and the Californios. But the Los Angeles battle turned out to be mainly of words. With very little active opposition, the Stars and Stripes were flown over the town, and on August 17, Stockton proclaimed California a territory of the United States. He named John Charles Frémont commandant of the territory.

Although neither Stockton nor Frémont knew it, General Stephen Watts Kearny was then marching overland to assume command of the war against Mexico.

This mix-up of command was to cause Captain Frémont much sorrow, and also disgrace and persecution. But, meanwhile, he received an appointment as Lieutenant Colonel in the United States Army and went confidently ahead with Commodore Stockton's orders.

He was proceeding with his men southward in

cold and rainy December weather when he learned of a plan to ambush the party. He turned off his route and entered Foxen Canyon and made camp.

William Benjamin Foxen—Don Julian to his Spanish friends—was an ex-sailor who had come into possession of thousands of acres of California land through marriage to a Spanish girl. His sympathies were with the Americans. His wife's emotions were mixed, but she knew that the men waiting hopefully at their gates might be killed if they were not shown the way over little-known San Marcos Pass, near Santa Barbara.

When she declared herself for the American cause, her husband and their oldest son, Guillermo, offered to guide Colonel Frémont over the pass.

The California Battalion entered Santa Barbara without bloodshed. Soon afterward a treaty was signed, and the so-called "war" came to an end.

9

Heartbreaking Days

WHEN GENERAL KEARNY arrived in California, there was an immediate clash between him and Commodore Stockton. Colonel Frémont, who had received his orders from Stockton, was in the middle of this quarrel. He took Stockton's part, and this fact angered Kearny, who was still smarting over the cannon dispute.

Kearny had received official orders, therefore he was entitled to assume control. His first move

was to strip Colonel Frémont of his title of Civil
Governor of California. This move was indignity
enough, but Kearny was still not satisfied. He
ordered Colonel Frémont to surrender the surveying equipment that had been a part of his life since,
at the age of twenty-four, he first began work with
Nicollet.

Those were heartbreaking days. So were the
weeks and months that followed, when he was
tried and sentenced to be dismissed from military
service because of his part in the California affair.

Public sentiment was strong for him, and President Polk pardoned him—without, however, dis-
missing some of the charges against him—but

Colonel Frémont, deeply humiliated, resigned his command, folded the uniform he had worn with distinction, and laid it away.

"He was ground to bits," his friends commented, "between the ambitions of two strong men."

He had scaled the loftiest peaks, only to be pulled down by men who seemed determined to destroy him.

Following the court-martial the Frémonts decided to move to California and to make their future home there.

"John bought land in the Santa Cruz Mountains," Mrs. Frémont told her friends. "We'll live there."

Later they were to learn that the friend who was to buy the land with the money Frémont intrusted to him, had betrayed his trust. He had bought the Santa Cruz land for himself and supposedly worthless Mariposa acreage for Frémont.

Before the Frémonts were ready to leave for the West, a group of influential men who were interested in building a railroad across the nation proposed that Frémont head an expedition which they would finance. He would not have to return to the East, therefore it would be a less expensive effort for him.

He had laid away his uniform but not his love for exploring and map making. He wanted to get back to the far view and the campfires at night. However, to do this would mean that Mrs. Frémont and Lily would have to make the trip to Panama, then over the Isthmus on mule back without him.

Mrs. Frémont urged him to accept the new commission.

She went with him as far as Kaw's Landing. Major Cummins, Agent at the Delaware Indian Agency, provided a log cabin for them. It was comfortable, in a primitive fashion. Though it had a dirt floor and homemade furniture, it had a huge fireplace at one end, and there was always game to be found for food.

It was October before John Frémont had his surveying party assembled, but he was not afraid of cold weather. Following the Santa Fé Trail, he marched across Kansas and into Colorado.

His first disappointment came when he reached Bent's Fort.

"Have you heard from Carson?" he asked Thomas Fitzpatrick, who was there to greet him. "And are you ready to come with me?"

Fitzpatrick shook his head.

"It's no to both questions," he said regretfully. "I've been appointed Indian Agent here, and Kit says he's going to stay with his family this winter. He's getting older, you know," he added. "Me, too. I don't take to snow and ice like I used to."

Frémont realized, with a sudden pang, that he, too, was getting older. He had always said surveying was for young men under forty. He was then thirty-five.

"Old Bill Williams is in Pueblo," a man at the trading post told Frémont. "He's just getting over a bullet shot in his arm, but he might be able to go. He's been a good guide, but he's sixty or so now."

Frémont rode on to Pueblo and went to see the old man.

"I'll go, but I warn you! This looks like a bad year. Lots of snow up above, and you've got mighty high mountains to cross," the old man grumbled.

Frémont had never seen such a winter as the one of 1848. Blizzards whipped the men so hard that they could not stand up against the force.

Their mules and horses slipped and fell. Before the men had a chance to struggle over the Sangre de Cristo Mountains, a great part of the corn they had shucked and shelled at Pueblo for horse and mule feed was scattered along the route.

It was mid-December when they reached the Rio Grande River. There, Williams and Frémont clashed. Williams insisted that the expedition move directly west across the lofty San Juan Mountains. Frémont's instincts told him to go north to the Gunnison River.

When Alexander Godey, one of his best men and a friend of Carson, agreed with Williams, Frémont yielded, moving west.

This error in judgment cost him the lives of eleven of his men, and almost ended his own career for all time.

When it became evident that the men were unable to cross the mountains in that frigid weather, Frémont sent Old Bill Williams and three other men to Taos for help. While they were gone, he moved the remnant of the party back down to the Rio Grande, and when there was no evidence that rescue was imminent after sixteen long days, he took four men and started to Taos.

They found the first expedition, one dead and the other men too weak to go on. After giving them all the supplies they had, the rescuers went on to Taos, where Kit Carson gave them aid and helped to organize a rescue party.

Alexander Godey led the new group back after the stranded men, as Frémont's left side and leg had frozen, and he could not ride.

However, as soon as he was able to sit in the saddle, he outfitted another expedition of about twenty-five men, sixty mules and horses, and rode south into Apache land.

Somewhere in the vicinity of Tucson, Arizona, one of the guides shouted, "Injuns! Injuns!" A large band of Apaches had appeared on a ridge not far away.

Since Apaches were noted for their savagery, Frémont knew that this was no time to "show the white feather" of fear.

He ordered the others to wait, and he wheeled his horse and sped to meet the Indians. He took them by surprise by telling them that he had been looking for them. He explained that he was going after supplies to barter with them for horses, but where could he meet them on his return?

Offguard, they told him where to meet them, then they went their way. The expedition left that area with haste.

When they reached the Colorado River, they

learned about the gold strike in California. A group of Mexicans was on its way to the mines. In the wild hope that there might be gold on the land he thought he had purchased, Frémont hired the Mexicans to work for him.

When he reached San Diego, he found that Mrs. Frémont and Lily had been delayed at Panama because of overloaded ships that were filled with gold seekers. He, therefore, continued to San Francisco, where he and his family were eventually reunited.

Meanwhile, Frémont had learned that he owned no land in the lovely Santa Clara Valley, but that there was indeed gold on the rocky Mariposa land which his "friend" had purchased for him! Consequently, he sent the Mexicans there to mine for him while he tried to find a house in which to live.

Prices in San Francisco at that time were sky-high. Every house was taken. He finally found quarters in Monterey and moved his family there.

At last, after all his troubles, his sadness over the court-martial; the terrible winter he had endured; his injured leg and side, fortune smiled on him. Almost overnight the Frémonts had become millionaires. Under the beds and in the small attic of the little Monterey adobe, were bags and bags of gold! Gold from the Mariposa!

Frémont's name had become respected in California. The Californians thought of him as a man who had helped to bring California under the protection of the Stars and Stripes. They knew of his bravery in crossing the wilderness. When a senator for the new state-to-be was needed, many of them immediately selected Frémont.

Two men were chosen, one for the short term and one for the long term. According to tradition, the two men were to draw straws for the long term. Unfortunately, William M. Gwin drew the long straw. Frémont would serve only a few weeks, but at least, he would enjoy the prestige of being California's first senator.

He went to Washington in knee-high miner's boots, rough western trousers, fringed buckskin jacket, and his familiar trademark — the old slouch hat. Everyone stared at him. He was graying now, but his black eyes still seemed to be piercing the distances. Though he walked with a slight limp, he carried himself with soldierly erectness.

Before returning to California, the Frémonts bought mining equipment, because a vein of gold had been found on their Mariposa land.

Again they sailed from New York for the Panama crossing of the Isthmus and the steamer up the coast and "home," as they now called California. This time they bought a house in San Francisco, and there their son, John Charles, was born. But the growing boom city that had replaced placid little Yerba Buena was in the grip of lawless men. People were killed on main streets in broad daylight. Fires were started by arsonists.

Frémont was at the mines when fire flared on their street. Mrs. Frémont, Lily, and the baby escaped, but their home burned to the ground, and that night — with other homeless people — they slept in the sand dunes.

Mrs. Frémont was severely shocked because of the experience. When her illness continued, John Charles Frémont made a decision. What was gold compared to the welfare of his wife and children? Why could they not have a genuine vacation together? After all, they had not even had a honeymoon, as he had spent most of his time on various trips.

"I have a Christmas present for us all," he announced in December. "We're going to Europe for a year."

10

He Had Served His Country Well

THE NAME "FRÉMONT" had become almost as well-known in Europe as it was in the United States. The Frémonts were royally treated abroad, and had a marvelous time, especially in France. But when they returned to the United States, their friends began to urge Frémont to continue his plan to chart the route of an East-West railroad through the center of the United States.

"Exploring is for the young," Frémont told his

wife. "I'm forty. My leg pains me at times. I doubt whether I have the endurance."

The call to action proved stronger than his reasoning. With his own money he outfitted a fifth expedition and set out in September, 1853, to find the pass through the Rockies which he had hoped to find during his almost disastrous journey with Old Bill Williams.

This time he succeeded. Hard luck hit the party in Utah, however, and only a fortunate meeting with a band of friendly Ute Indians saved them from starvation. Though they had made it safely through the Rockies and on to Salt Lake, Frémont did not undertake the Sierra Nevadas that winter. Instead of going over them through the pass that he had already established, he traveled south along the eastern ramparts of the mountains, crossing at the lower, southern point.

Returning seven months later, as he had promised, he was satisfied in one respect: He knew that, sooner or later, someone would lay shining rails across the Rockies and the Sierra Nevadas, roughly following the Kansas City-Denver-Salt Lake-Sacramento line that he had explored.

The Civil War erupted, changing plans on a

national scale. President Lincoln called for volunteers and commissioned John Charles Frémont a major general. Once more Frémont donned the uniform of the Union as one of the four major generals in the United States Army.

For all his brilliance and force, and perhaps

because he was more accustomed to giving orders than to taking them, his military life was as unrewarding as his political life. He had been nominated for President of the United States in 1856; he had lived to see cities spring up where once his campfires had flickered in the uninhabited wilderness; he had lived to see the West, which he had helped to open up, enriched by millions of home seekers, but as the circumstances of others improved, his own affairs grew steadily worse.

Bad investments, legal difficulties with his California mines, his failure to build a railroad with his own funds — all these factors contributed to one final blow. In 1870 he was not only penniless and in debt, but he was ill. His fabulous fortune had melted like the snows of summer.

America did not forget John Charles Frémont. When, in 1878, he had regained his strength, President Rutherford B. Hayes appointed him to the position of Territorial Governor of Arizona.

He and Mrs. Frémont, accompanied by their daughter — the boys, Charles and Frank were in school in the East — made the trip across the continent on a train. They stayed in San Francisco a few days, then rode another train from Los Angeles to

Yuma, Arizona, the end of the line.

Three Army ambulances met them at that point. Their luggage was stowed in two of them, and the Frémonts rode in the third, enjoying being taken by six-mule teams to Prescott in the pines.

Prescott, at that time the capital of Arizona, was a frontier town, with boardwalks and log cabins, high winds and friendly people. It reminded Governor and Mrs. Frémont of Yerba Buena and young San Francisco, although there was not the hustle and bustle of the latter.

Governor Frémont lost no time in securing rid-

ing horses from Fort Whipple, a few miles away. He and Lily enjoyed golden days riding in the forests and pines of northern Arizona. Frémont saw the possibilities of an irrigation project and spent his time at home drawing up plans for it.

Mrs. Frémont was less happy. The altitude affected her health, and she was forced to return to the East. Frémont soon resigned his governorship and followed her.

He was now an old man as years go, and he was tired. He had lived through one of the most exciting periods in the history of the United States. He had served his country to the best of his ability. Now he felt there was one more duty he should perform. For the youth of the future, he should make a record of his life.

It was a long, hard, time-consuming task, but he finished his *Memoirs* before, at seventy-eight, he closed his eyes in the long sleep, his search for adventure at an end.

But America continued to remember him. His monuments stretch from the Great Lakes to the Pacific in many towns named "Frémont." And Frémont Peak, second highest in the Wind River Range, is in huge Frémont County, Wyoming.

Probably one of his happiest moments came when the United States Government presented him with a pension of six thousand dollars a year, "In recognition of services rendered to his country."

Bibliography

BRANDON, WILLIAM. *John Charles Frémont, the Man and the Mountain.* New York: William Morrow & Co., Inc., 1955.

BURT, OLIVE. *Camel Express.* Philadelphia: The John C. Winston Company, 1954.

CARLSON, VADA F. *This Is Our Valley.* Los Angeles: Westernlore Press, 1959.

DELLENBAUGH, F. S. *Breaking the Wilderness.* New York and London: G. P. Putnam's Sons, 1904.

————. *Frémont and '49.* New York and London: G. P. Putnam's Sons, 1914.

ELLIS, EDWARD S. *Life of Kit Carson.* New York: Grosset & Dunlap, Inc., 1899.

FERGUSSON, ERNA. *Our Southwest.* New York: Alfred A. Knopf, Inc., 1940.

GOODWIN, CARDINAL LEONIDAS. *John Charles Frémont, an Explanation of His Career.* Palo Alto, Calif.: Stanford University Press, 1930.

FRÉMONT, BREVET CAPTAIN J. C. *Report of the Exploring Expedition to the Rocky Mountains in the Year 1846, and to Oregon and North California in the Years 1843-44, 1845.* Washington, D.C.: Executive Document 166, Blair and Rives, Printers.

FRÉMONT, JOHN CHARLES. *Memoirs of My Life.* Chicago and New York: Bedford, Clark, and Company, 1887.

LAVENDER, DAVID. *Bent's Fort.* New York: Doubleday & Company, Inc., 1954. Now in reprint by Peter Smith, Gloucester, Mass.

NEVINS, ALLAN. *Frémont, Pathmarker of the West* (Vol. I). New York: Frederick Ungar Publishing Co., Inc., 1939, 1955.

————. *Frémont, Pathmarker of the West* (Vol. II). New York: Frederick Ungar Publishing Co., Inc., 1955.

————. *Frémont, the West's Greatest Adventurer.* New York and London: Harper and Brothers, 1928.

SABIN, EDW. L. *Kit Carson Days.* Chicago: A. C. McClurg & Co., 1914.

STONE, IRVING. *Immortal Wife.* New York: Doubleday & Company, Inc., 1948.

————. *Men to Match My Mountains.* New York: Doubleday & Company, Inc., 1956.

UPHAM, CHARLES WENTWORTH. *Life, Explorations and Public Service of John Charles Frémont.* Boston: Ticknor and Fields, 1856.

WYLLYS, RUFUS K. *Arizona, the History of a Frontier State.* Phoenix, Arizona: Hobson and Herr, 1950.

Index

A

Abert, John J., head of U.S. Topographical
  Engineers' Corps, 127, 138
Abert Lake, 127
Alvarado, Juan Bautista, California
  Governor, 144
Apaches, 157
Arkansas River, 112, 142
Astor, John Jacob, 63

B

Bear Flag Revolt, 146
Bear River, 114, 146
Benton, Jessie, wife of John Charles
  Frémont, 63-72
Benton, Randolph, 105
Benton, Thomas Hart, 61-63, 66-69, 71-73,
  106-7
Bent's Fort, 112, 136, 154
Bent, William, 136
Bernier, Jean Baptiste, 115
Big Snake River, 79
Big Sandy River, 96
Blue Earth River, 46
Blue Mountains, 122
Bridger, Jim, 76, 86, 87
Brown's Hole, 79
Buffalo, 43, 44, 51-5, 84, 85

C

Cache Camp, 94, 102
California, 108-9-10, 134, 148, 161, 166
California Battalion, 147
Californios, 108, 110, 134
Carson, Christopher (Kit), mountain man
  and guide to Frémont, 76-79, 82-85,
  92-94, 112-113, 116, 130-34, 136,
  141-43, 155-56
Cascade Mountains, 123
Castro, José, 144
Cecilia, Frémont's Creole girl friend,
  19-22, 36
Charleston College, 18, 19, 29
Charleston, South Carolina, Frémont
  entered school there, 13, 24
Cherokee Indians, 30-33
Cheyenne Indians, 87
Christmas Lake, 127
Civil War, 164

Colorado, 113, 154
Colorado River, 158
Columbia River, 109, 110, 123, 129
Continental Divide, 76, 96, 114
Cottonwood River, 45

D

Deer Creek, 94
Des Moines River, 70
Deschutes River, 123
Delaware Indians, 142
Delaware Indian Agency, 154

E

Emmons, George Foster, 109, 123

F

Feather River, 146
Fishing Falls, 122
Fitzpatrick, Thomas (Broken Hand), 76,
  112, 114, 115, 122, 131, 155
Foxen Canyon, 149
Foxen, Guillermo, 149
Foxen, William Benjamin (Don Julian), 149
Fort Hall, 115, 121
Fort Laramie, 86, 93, 102-3
Fort Pierre, 49-50
Fort Vancouver, 123
Fort Whipple, 168
Frémont, Anne (Whiting), mother of
  John Charles Frémont, 11, 13
Frémont, Charles, father of John Charles
  Frémont, 11, 13
Frémont County, Wyoming, 168
Frémont, Jessie Benton, wife of John
  Charles Frémont, 72
Frémont, John Charles, 9, 13, 16, 17,
  enters college, 18; expelled, 22; first
  surveying job, 23-4; cruise, 26-9; receives
  degree from Charleston College, 29;
  appointed second lientenant U.S. Topographical Engineers' Corps, 30; Cherokee Country experience, 30-3; first
  expedition with Nicollet, 35-9; 45; first
  meeting with Sioux Indians, 50-1; buffalo
  hunt, 52-6; second trip with Nicollet,
  41-60; meets Jessie Benton, 63-5; court-
  ship and marriage, 66-72; named to
  succeed Nicollet, 75; heads expedition,

meets Kit Carson, 76; climbs Frémont
Peak, 76-99; success make him national
hero, 104; 1843 expedition approved,
105; first baby (Lily) born, 105; moves
to St. Louis, 106; Kearny lends cannon
for trip, 110; Salt Lake, 117-119; reaches
Western Slope, 122; crosses Sierra
Nevada mountains, 132; Sutter's Fort,
133, trouble over cannon, 138; third
expedition approved by Congress, 140;
General Winfield Scott presents Frémont
with commission as captain, 140; Third
Expedition charts Salt Lake, 142; spends
winter in California, 144; Bear Flag
Revolt, 146; heads California Battalion,
148; named commandant of California
Territory, 148; clash with Kearny, 151;
court-martial, 153; Frémonts move to
California, 153; Frémont undertakes
winter crossing of Colorado mountains,
loses men, freezes leg, 154; learns of gold
strike in California, 159; gold found on
Mariposa holdings, 160; serves as California's first senator, short term, 164;
San Francisco home burns, 162; in
Europe, 163; private survey for railroad,
163-4; nominated for President of U.S.,
166; given rank of major general by
President Lincoln, 165; appointed
Territorial Governor of Arizona, 167;
resigned, 168; died at age 78, 168.
Frémont Peak, 99, 100
Frenière, Louison, 57

G
Gillespie, Archibald H., 145
Godey, Alexander, 156
Great Basin (of Salt Lake), 135
Great Plains, 11
Great Salt Lake, 110, 114, 119
Green River, 96
Gros Ventre Indians, 87
Gwin, William M., 161

H
Harrison, William H., 66-7
Hassler, Ferdinand, 35, 37, 39, 62, 68
Hayes, Rutherford B., 166
Hiwassee River, 33, 34, 36

Humboldt, Baron Friedrich Heinrich
Alexander von, 142
Humboldt River, 142

I
Isthmus of Panama, 161

J
Jackson Hole, 79
James River, 49

K
Kansas, 154
Kansas River, 77, 79, 80
Kaw's Landing, 154
Klamath Lake, 125-26
Klamath Indians, 126

L
Larkin, Thomas O., 145
Lajuenesse, Basil, 77, 80, 81, 87, 97, 115
Lewis and Clark, 63, 85
Lincoln, Abraham, 165
Little Sandy River, 96
Little Wind River, 95
Los Angeles, 148

M
Mariposa, 153, 160, 161
Maxwell, Lucien Bonaparte, 77, 86, 142
Mexican Territory, 110, 134, 144
Mexicans, 159
Mexico, 110, 140
Minnesota River, 41-4, 46
Mississippi River, 12, 25, 41, 43
Missouri River, 11, 12, 25, 35, 41, 49, 51,
63, 73, 102, 136
Mission San Juan Bautista, 144
Mitchell, John W., 16, 22
Monte del Diablo, Devil Mountain, 130
Montgomery, John B., 147
Monterey, 147

N
Natchez, training sloop of war, 26
Nevada, 142, 143
Nicollet, Joseph Nicholas, French astron-
omer and geologist, 35, 37, 39, 40, 44-6,
50-1, 56, 58, 60, 62, 75
North Platte, 101

O
Oregon, 144
Oregon Trail, 113, 121-2
Owens, Richard, 141, 142

P
Pacific Coast, 108
Panama, 154
Pike, Zebulon M., 63
Platte River, 83
Poinsett, Joel Roberts, 26, 34, 35, 69, 70
Polk, James Knox, 139, 152
Prairie du Chien, 59
Prescott, 167
Preuss, Charles, 77, 82, 86, 115
Proclamation of War with Mexico, 147
Pyramid Lake, 129

R
Red Pipestone Quarry, 45, 48
Renville, Joseph, 46
Richmond, Virginia, 13
Rio Grande River, 156
Robertson, Dr. Charles, 16, 17, 18, 21

S
Sacramento River, 144
Sacramento Valley, 109, 130, 133
St. Louis, Mo., 12, 15, 37, 38, 40, 42, 48,
    59, 61, 76, 78, 101, 105, 106, 107, 136
Salmon River, 121
San Diego, 147
San Francisco, 108, 160, 166
Sangre de Cristo Mountains, 156
San Joaquin Valley, 134
San Juan Bautista, 144
San Juan Mountains, 156
San Marcos Pass, 149
Santa Barbara, California, 149
Santa Clara Valley, 160
Santa Cruz Mountains, California, 153
Santa Fé Trail, 154
Savannah, Georgia, 13
"Savannah," 147
Scott, General Winfield, 140, 141
Schoolcraft, Henry Rowe, 24, 63
Sierra Nevada Mountains, 128, 129, 135,
    164

Sioux Indians, 41-4, 46, 50-1, 86-9, 91-2
Sloat, John Drake, 147
Smith, Jedediah, 63
Sonoma, California, 146
South Dakota, 49
South Pass (Wyo.), 76, 86, 96, 110, 114
Spanish Trail, 135
Stockton, Robert F., 147-8, 151
Summer Lake, 127
Sutter, John, 109
Sutter's Fort, 109, 133, 134
Sweetwater River, 87, 95

T
Taos, New Mexico, 136, 141, 156-57
Tehachapi Mountains, 135
Teton Mountains, 100
The Dalles, 123
Tucson, 157
Tyler, John, 74

U
U.S. Topographical Engineers' Corps, 29,
    34, 61, 104, 108, 124, 136
Utah Lake, 142
Ute Indians, 164

V
Van Buren, Martin, 34
Virgin River, 135

W
Walker, Joseph Reddeford, 135-36, 142-43
Walker's Lake, 143
Walker's Pass, 143
Walla Walla Valley, 122
Whiting, Thomas W., 13
Whitman, Marcus, 122
Wilkes, Charles, 108
Willamette River, 109
Williams, Bill, 155-56
Williams, W. S., 30
Wind River, 95
Wind River Mountains, 95
Wyoming (territory), 83

Y
Yerba Buena, 108, 162, 168
Yuma, Arizona, 167

About the Author

Vada Carlson writes of the American West from the viewpoint of a westerner, a journalist, a poet, and an historian. Born in Nebraska, raised in Wyoming, and now residing in Arizona, she has lived near Indian reservations most of her life and has acquired a deep love and knowledge of western lore and Indian cultures — especially of the Sioux, the Shoshone and Arapahoe, the Navaho and the Apaches. She is the author of a number of books and of countless newspaper and magazine articles and stories, which have brought her honors and awards.

About the Artist

A native of Detroit, Michigan, and now a resident of Florida, William Orr is especially known for his paintings of horses. This interest began in his youth with sketching horses while working in a livery stable and at rodeos. It was continued during World War II when he served in the Army Remount Service. Mr. Orr studied art at the Detroit Art Institute, the Kendal School of Design, the Art Students League of New York, and under Alexandre Zlatoff-Merski of Chicago and Carlos Merida of Mexico City.

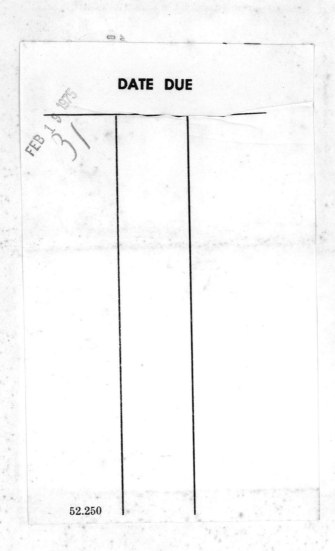